TRANSACTIONS

OF THE

AMERICAN PHILOSOPHICAL SOCIETY

HELD AT PHILADELPHIA

FOR PROMOTING USEFUL KNOWLEDGE

NEW SERIES—VOLUME 62, PART 5

1972

THE MAJOR POLITICAL ISSUES OF THE JACKSONIAN PERIOD AND THE DEVELOPMENT OF PARTY LOYALTY IN CONGRESS, 1830-1840

DAVID J. RUSSO

Associate Professor of History, McMaster University

THE AMERICAN PHILOSOPHICAL SOCIETY

INDEPENDENCE SQUARE

PHILADELPHIA

MAY, 1972

Library of Congress Catalog
Card Number 72–76612
International Standard Book Number 0–87169–625–8

THE MAJOR POLITICAL ISSUES OF THE JACKSONIAN PERIOD AND THE DEVELOPMENT OF PARTY LOYALTY IN CONGRESS, 1830–1840

DAVID J. RUSSO

CONTENTS

INTRODUCTION

We know much more about the development of political parties than any previous generation of historians claimed to know. And a great deal of our understanding comes from studies published within the last fifteen years. The work of Noble Cunningham, David Fischer, Richard McCormick, Lee Benson, Joel Silbey, Thomas Alexander, and Richard Hofstadter—to mention just those who have dealt with the period before the Civil War—has clearly revealed the structure and functions of the institution which is commonly believed to have made the American political system operative and viable. Such subjects as the nature of party organization, the differences between the origins and development of the first and second party systems, the impact of party on congressional voting, and the rise of a "legitimate" opposition in Congress have been analyzed in considerable depth.[1]

Indeed, the most recent synthesizer of the Jacksonian period warns against an overemphasis on party. Stressing the pragmatic, heterogeneous, and non-ideological character of the two major parties, Edward Pessen points to the sporadic third-party developments as evidence that many important issues were not dealt with by the Democrats and the Whigs at all. The implication is that American society contained a political system which, by its nature, could not cope effectively with problems which many specific groups (such as the poor, the insane, prisoners, slaves, Indians, laborers, children, and women) in the society confronted. If one adds, as Pessen does, a portrait of the Jacksonian politician as opportunist *par excellence*, one who cared far more about winning office and wielding power than in applying principles or even being politically consistent, then politics becomes a game whose players are characteristically motivated by unattractive personal considerations and not by concern for the interests of a locality or the nation.[2] And if those areas in which the federal government *did* legislate—such as banking, tariff, and internal improvements—are not regarded as having been of vital importance to the economic development of the United States, a view which Pessen takes, one must seriously wonder about the propriety of the current focus, not only on the party system, but on national politics generally. One is almost left with a picture of a society whose emergence was not guided in significant ways by government.

This approach can also be taken too far, however. For instance, perhaps one reason the major parties shunned certain problems was because these matters did not concern a majority of the voters. Reform movements on behalf of peace, criminals, the insane, and women undoubtedly excited small groups who worked assiduously for the cause, but hardly provoked widespread popular interest. With the superiority of the white race a cardinal tenet of popular thought, it is not surprising that there was virtually no opposition to the constitutional sanction of slavery in the States

---

[1] Noble Cunningham, Jr., *The Jeffersonian Republicans: The Formation of Party Organization, 1789–1801* (Chapel Hill, 1957) and *The Jeffersonian Republicans in Power: Party Operations, 1801–1809* (Chapel Hill, 1963); David Fischer, *The Revolution of American Conservatism: The Federalist Party in the Era of Jeffersonian Democracy* (New York, 1965); Richard McCormick, *The Second American Party System: Party Formation in the Jacksonian Era* (Chapel Hill, paperback edition, 1966); Lee Benson, *The*

Concept of Jacksonian Democracy: New York as a Test Case (New York, paperback edition, 1964); Joel Silbey, *The Shrine of Party: Congressional Voting Behavior, 1841–1852* (Pittsburgh, 1967); Thomas B. Alexander, *Sectional Stress and Party Strength: A Study of Roll-call Voting Patterns in the United States House of Representatives, 1836–1860* (Nashville, 1967); Richard Hofstadter, *The Idea of a Party System: The Rise of Legitimate Opposition in the United States, 1780–1840* (Berkeley and Los Angeles, 1969).

[2] Edward Pessen, *Jacksonian America: Society, Personality, and Politics* (Homewood, Illinois, 1969).

3

or to the government's policy of Indian removal and later civilization of the tribes. The utter ineffectuality of the Liberty party—which was frankly anti-slavery—in 1844 was sufficient warning, if any were needed, for the major parties to avoid that position. Opposition to Jackson's removal policy in the early 1830's was over means, not ends. Since the "Civilized Tribes" were living in Georgia by right of earlier, valid treaties and had already adopted the ways of white Americans, why move them? Some matters, such as aid to "public improvements" (education, roads, canals, rivers, harbors), it was widely felt, were the proper concern of state government. And though national politicians debated for decades the propriety and desirability of congressional support for these projects, the highly irregular aid which in fact was granted should not be allowed to obscure continuous programs by state governments. Congressional power to regulate the currency and raise revenue led some nationalist-minded politicians to favor the formation of a government-sponsored bank and a high schedule of tariff duties, both of which would aid the development of a non-colonial, industrial economy. And, though the actual importance of these measures to American economic development can legitimately be debated, no one can deny that the issues which arose were of great concern to politicians and voters alike. Hostility to protection was the direct cause of the nullification controversy in 1832–1833. Disagreement over the government's proper relationship to banks and the currency resulted in the deepest and most continuous ideological and party divisions of any issue between 1789 and 1860.

It is also overly simplistic to argue that politicians were opportunistic and selfish. They were also, at certain times and in particular places, highly loyal to political organizations. Van Buren's "Regency" is only the best known example of a state "machine" whose members' highest concern was for consistency and faithfulness to what leaders in Albany decided was the *party's* position.[3] Similar organizations existed in such states as New Hampshire, Massachusetts, Vermont, Virginia, North Carolina, South Carolina, Georgia, and Missouri.[4] McCormick's study emphasizes the indispensability of loyalty and obedience in the formation of parties in the states during the 1830's. Furthermore, Silbey's and Alexander's studies both demonstrate that party allegiance was an important factor in congressional voting patterns as early as the mid-1830's. Putting all these studies together, the only valid conclusion is that the parties which formed in the late 1820's and the 1830's were, by the middle of the decade, in a

position to demand a great deal of their congressional adherents. Representatives and senators were not only nominated and elected as Whigs and Democrats, but they were also expected to *vote* as Whigs and Democrats.

It seems incontestable that party loyalty has to be *one* factor in any comprehensive explanation of political behaviour during the life of the second-party system. And yet what is equally obvious is that not all issues evoked the same degree of "party" voting. Unfortunately neither Silbey nor Alexander is concerned with some rather vexing questions: *Why* did certain matters, such as the banking and currency issue, bring forth a far greater display of party allegiance than others, such as internal improvement expenditures? *Why* did some issues become known as "party" and others as distinctly "non-party" matters? How did congressmen themselves explain their uneven relationship to party? What explains the failure of certain congressmen to support party positions even on questions which were obviously regarded as party issues by virtually everyone? Surely numerous charts and graphs precisely delineating the extent of the allegiance of individual congressment answers what should be only the first question in a line of inquiry. Concerned only with the *measurement* of party loyalty, Silbey and Alexander do not go on to *explain* the phenomenon.[4a]

Any adequate explanation of the role party loyalty played during the 1830–1860 period has to involve an assessment of the various kinds of influences which operated upon congressmen: petitions, instructions, letters from constituents, positions taken in the most recent campaign, congressional committee reports, presidential messages, statements of party leaders and the party journals located in Washington, the pe-

---

[3] Michael Wallace, "Changing Concepts of Party in the United States: New York, 1815–1828," *Amer. Hist. Rev.* **74,** 2 (December, 1968): pp. 453–491.

[4] McCormick, *The Second American Party System,* pp. 36–49, 54–62, 69–76, 178–209, 236–246, 304–310.

[4a] In fact, Alexander presents his study as a kind of research tool for scholars of the period: "It is not the purpose of this appraisal to pursue all relevant conclusions that might be indicated by the roll-call analysis offered. One of the reasons for making available these data and the patterns exposed by certain research designs is to furnish conveniently prepared information for use by students of the period. This appraisal seeks only to explore some of the promising avenues for question framing and further investigation." Alexander, *Sectional Stress and Party Strength,* p. 110. Unfortunately, the usefulness of Alexander's study is considerably reduced by his failure to analyze the Senate's voting patterns for these same years.

Silbey's "aims are limited: to apply one kind of quantitative analysis to one level of the political arena over one period of time, [thereby] . . . carefully measuring how much either sectional or party considerations affected a prime reflector of public opinion—Congressional roll-call voting." Silbey, *The Shrine of Party,* pp. viii–ix.

Actually, the emphasis in these two studies differs. Silbey is anxious to show that nationalizing influences, such as party loyalty, were very much in evidence until the end of the second party system, in the mid-1850's. Alexander investigates a considerably longer period, and, while corroborating Silbey's evidence, he is also concerned about the sectionalization of the parties during the 1850's, something which, of course, culminated in the events of 1861.

culiarities of the party organizations or the overall political situation in particular states. All were in evidence, and, in the aggregate, reveal why there was never total unanimity among either the Whigs or the Democrats in Congress.

As Alexander clearly demonstrates it was during the 1830's, not the 1840's, when the impact of party on voting first manifested itself. The period dealt with in Silbey's book, 1840–1852, is obviously the most stable one from the standpoint of the two major parties, and thus the one in which they would be expected to have exerted the most influence on the political process generally. And yet it would be a mistake to regard the previous decade as a time in which the formation of organizations was the only significant development relating to the institution which played, as much then as now, a central role in the life of American government. Some years before both parties were uniformly organized in *all* areas of the nation—McCormick fixes the date at 1840—it is quite clear that party identification was a factor in the positions congressmen adopted on issues, but far more on some than on others. In this article, an investigation of the growth of party loyalty within the major parties of Congress will be undertaken, focused on questions ignored in the studies done by Alexander and Silbey.

CONGRESSIONAL ATTITUDES ON THE SUBJECT OF PARTY LOYALTY

Though nominations, campaigns, and elections were under the direction of parties in large areas of the nation by 1832, and everywhere but the most western states by 1836, congressmen throughout the decade voiced their opposition to party loyalty being the basis for positions on matters discussed or acted upon while Congress was in session. Thomas Hall, himself elected as a Democrat from North Carolina before the development of a Whig opposition there, told his colleagues in the House: "Would to God...we could have but one party—one great party—all the members of which, instead of scrambling for place and public money, should be found vieing with each other in disinterested efforts to promote the public good." [5] Another Southerner, Robert Hunter (a Virginia Democrat) added to this sentiment when he said in June, 1838, several years after the South had developed a two-party system:

For myself, I am governed by no party motives upon such a question as this [the Independent Treasury bill of 1838]. I feel myself proudly above them. In saying this I mean no disrespect to those who adopt the rules of party action; they have the authority of eminent names, perhaps of public opinion itself, to sustain them in the propriety of submitting their conduct to such rules.

For one, however, I never will consent to merge all individuality of sentiment and action in the great mass of party. I never will take upon myself that allegiance which should bind me to obey the will of a party, even though the obedience involved a sacrifice of the wishes and dearest interests of those who sent me here. As the agent of my constituents, I will either represent them, according to the sense of right when I know it, or will give way for another who may do it with a safer conscience. But beyond this, and when they leave me a free agent, I acknowledge no responsibility to any but to that being who gave me a conscience for my guide. [6]

Others also emphasized that their primary duty was to be loyal to the interests of their constituents, even if such a commitment contradicted their party's position on an issue. [7] Those who spoke in this way were not always Southerners. William Wick, Democrat from Indiana, said at the end of the decade: "I am always sorry to see any question embarrassed by political considerations. It is fatal to all fair and useful legislation to bring general politics to bear on particular questions. Particular questions ought to depend upon their particular merits." [8] This concern that party politics somehow be kept out of Congress was expressed in another way, perhaps unwittingly, by Senator Thomas Benton, Democrat from Missouri, when he characterized the speeches delivered by the Whigs on the Independent Treasury bill of 1838 as having "been such as might be expected at the partisan encounters of the hustings, on the stump, or at barbecue dinners, in the course of an electioneering campaign for an elective office, and not such as would be looked for in a parliamentary discussion of a legislative measure." [9] And as late as 1840, J. W. Allen, a Whig from Ohio, when speaking on the bill that divided Congress along party lines to a greater extent than any previous measure, still thought it appropriate to say:

If we come here with our minds fixed or opinions immovable, our ears closed against all argument, we can hardly be entitled to the appellation of a deliberative assembly. Whatever weight may be attached to the proposition . . ., for myself I do not feel its force to any embarrassing extent. I was elected as an opponent of the Administration and its measures generally, but whether I should support or oppose this or that particular measure, neither my constituents nor myself knew with certainty. They knew I was originally and strongly opposed to the bill, but since that time, now almost two years, that judgment was passed upon me and upon that, many occurrences may have taken place to induce a change in some individuals of the opinion then entertained, both by its friends and its enemies. [10]

---

[5] (May 19, 1832) *Register of Debates in Congress* (Washington, 1825–1837) 8: pp. 3067–3068. Henceforth cited as *Register of Debates*.

[6] (June 22, 1838) *Congressional Globe Containing the Debates and Proceedings of the U. S. Congress* (Washington, 1833–1873), 6 (appendix): p. 446. Henceforth cited as *Congressional Globe*.

[7] For example, Plummer, Democrat from Mississippi (March 31, 1834), *ibid*. 1: p. 279; and Hawes, Democrat from Kentucky (April (?), 1836), *ibid*. 3 (appendix): p. 347.

[8] (January 8, 1840) *ibid*. 8: p. 174.

[9] (March 14, 1838) *ibid*. 6 (appendix): p. 209.

[10] (June 24, 1840) *ibid*. 8 (appendix): p. 712.

Others frankly admitted their party allegiance while simultaneously asserting an independence of thought and action that was sometimes the result of choice, sometimes of force of circumstances. John W. Davis, an Indiana Democrat, was blunt: "Though a party man, he did not approve of this part of the Administration." But, he added, "He was not one of those plastic politicians whose only merit was their pliability." [11] On other occasions, congressmen gave expression to their anxiety about being loyal Jackson supporters at the same time that popular sentiment was against a position the President had taken. Pennsylvania—throughout the decade—was the classic case of a strongly Democratic state whose voters just as strongly opposed some of the major policies of the Jackson administrations. Senator McKean, instructed by his legislature to favor restoration of the bank deposits in 1834, told his colleagues that:

He was what he professed to be, the sincere friend of Andrew Jackson, though he detested many of the reptiles that were basking in the beams of his effulgence, and without authority, claim to speak in his name. But he was also on that floor the humble representative in part of the people of Pennsylvania; and if he understood their interest, and knew their will on questions of mere expediency, he would advocate the one, and obey the other, please or displease whom it might. He was a party man as far as conscience would permit. He abhorred and condemned alike, a captious opposition, and a blind and sycophantic devotion to any Administration. [12]

Four years earlier, another Pennsylvanian noted in the House debate on Jackson's veto of the Maysville Road bill that in his state both the President and internal improvements were favored. His constituents

would abide by both, waiting with confidence for the slow but certain process by which the system of improvements would universally prevail. The President had, in vetoing the bill, exercised only his Constitutional power, and he . . . and his constituents, in supporting it, were only exercising the power which the Constitution granted to them. [13]

Other representatives, while acknowledging their personal loyalty and friendship toward Jackson, especially in terms of commitment to his candidacy, were quite upset when opposition members of Congress twitted them about their failure to support the President on certain measures. Though still a devoted personal and political friend of Jackson, Joseph Isacks of Tennessee showed no hesitation in asserting that on the question of internal improvements "he differed from the President—and what of it? We have differed before. . . ." Jackson would despise anyone who would change his conviction because of the veto message. And even if he did not, Isacks would say: "I cannot help it; to you, Mr. President, I owe no responsibilities; to none but God and my

constituents do I acknowledge responsibility, and these I will discharge as I may." [14] This in 1830, several years before the major parties were fully organized throughout the country.

Similar sentiments were expressed during the debates on the bank-deposits issue during the spring of 1834, the first time a clear pattern of party loyalty was evident in Congress. Senator King, a Democrat from Alabama, sought to repel the charge made by opposition senators that supporters of the administration were servile party men:

This is not the first time the friends of the Administration have been taunted with subserviency to Executive views. I have hitherto disdained to notice it. . . . I was known to those who placed me here as the personal and political friend of General Jackson. I have given to his Administration a firm and zealous, if not able support, whenever in my judgment, the measures proposed were calculated to advance the general interests. . . . On other occasions I have differed with the views of the President, and frankly made known to him that difference—and little do those who know him suppose that thus to act either lessens his respect or diminishes his friendship for the individual. . . . Base subserviency can never win his respect or command his favor. [15]

Representative Franklin Plummer, an unaffiliated representative from Mississippi,

said that he would here take the occasion to repel a charge that had been made from a quarter which he did not think proper to name, because it might be a violation of order, that his course on this question "was the effect of party trammels," that he was "under the influence of decided party discipline," that he had "become a mere automaton," and disposed to surrender his judgment, and what he believed to be the best interests of the people of Mississippi, at the shrine of party. [16]

Gayton Osgood, the only Democrat in the entire Massachusetts congressional delegation at this time, admitted that, even though "I was nominated by the friends of the Administration; I was supported by the friends of the Administration; and I was finally chosen as an open and avowed friend of the Administration. . .," there were situations in which his party's campaign pledges would no longer be a guide for proper action:

If he has openly avowed his adherence to a political party, if he has been chosen with a knowledge on the part of his constituents of his political predilections, he may safely conclude that a concurrence with the measures of his party will not be obnoxious to those who elected him. But a new state of things may arise, unexpected events may happen, unforeseen measures may be proposed, a different course of policy may be instituted, and the vote that sanctioned his adherence to his party at the time of his election may fail to sustain him in this new juncture of events, and he will be compelled to resort to some other criterion to determine the wishes of his constituents. [17]

[11] (April 30, 1840) *ibid.* 8: p. 369.
[12] (June 18, 1834) *ibid.* 1: p. 462.
[13] (May 28, 1830) *Register of Debates* 6: p. 1147.
[14] (May 28, 1830) *ibid.* 6: p. 1147.
[15] (April 17, 1834) *Congressional Globe* 1: p. 323.
[16] (March 31, 1834) *ibid.* 1: p. 279.
[17] (May 5, 1834) *ibid.* 1: pp. 363–364.

By 1836, however, not everyone was upset by charges of subservience to party. Ratcliff Boon, long-time Democratic representative from Indiana, commented on the subject in a humorous way, suggesting the widespread recognition that the influence of party had received by that time:

> . . . Those who comprise the Jackson Party are denounced by the new born Whigs as "collar dogs". . . . I am proud of the title thus conferred by the Whigs of 1834. Dogs wearing the collar of their master, are generally considered to be a superior class of dogs, having the entire confidence of their masters. Sir, I am a *party* man, and one of the true collar dogs. . . . and am proud to wear the collar of such a man as Andrew Jackson, whose collar is the collar of *Democracy*. . . .[18]

Several years later, Alexander Duncan, Whig representative from Ohio, told his colleagues: "Almost on every question of a general nature, when and where it is possible to drag a party feeling, party facts, and party arguments into discussion, it is universally done. I know of no instance where this has not been the case." [19] By 1840, Senator Clay, a Democrat from Alabama, even invoked the importance of party unity as an inducement for Democrats to support the President on an issue that had never become primarily a party-oriented matter. Arguing that a party, "to act long together and remain united . . . must entertain and act upon some common principles, and for common objects," Clay urged his colleagues to remain faithful to the strict constructionist principle of their party and oppose an appropriation for the continuation of the national road, as President Van Buren had.[20]

As congressmen gradually became accustomed to party voting they occasionally reflected on what they perceived to have been the nature and history of parties in the United States. Since they were obviously in a second party era, it was natural to try to have some perspective on the whole subject of parties. The sporadic surveys and analyses presented in the midst of debate were quite superficial, especially when compared to the rather penetrating remarks about the growing influence of party in the thirties. The only plausible explanation for this discrepancy is that politicians offered such explanations only when they were anxious to provide historic justification for the positions, constitutional interpretations, and images which their party wished to project. As if borrowing from De Tocqueville's highly schematic and simplistic analysis of the differences between the two major parties, administration supporters presented a clear and fundamental division between Federalist-Whigs and Republicans-Democrats, whether defined as aristocratic versus democratic or commercial versus agrarian. As Franklin Plummer, an independent representative from Mississippi put it:

> The question before the people of the United States [involving the deposits issue of 1834] is the same now . . . that it has ever been since the adoption of the Constitution, between the Federalist and the Republican—between the aristocracy and democracy—between those who are in favor of enlarging the powers of the general government, by implication, and those who are for confining it within the limits prescribed by the Constitution. Gentlemen disguise it as they would, that . . . was the real state of the question.[21]

Four years later, during the debate over the independent treasury bill, Senator Bedford Brown, Democrat of North Carolina, repeated this analysis, and added:

> These leading characteristics, then, existing between the two great parties, and separating them by a line plain and broad, had been perceptible on all the important public questions which had, from that time to this agitated the country. . . .
> Who, he would ask, were the supporters mainly of the present Administration? They were to be found mostly among the class of citizens, engaged in peaceful and honorable pursuits of agriculture. . . .
> Where, on the contrary, were the opponents of the Administration to be found? Chiefly, he believed, in cities and towns; and, although he did not doubt but that many among that kind of population were as patriotic and devoted to the cause of the country . . . yet a very large portion of them were necessarily dependent on the smiles and favors of that class . . . which controlled the machinery of [the money system][22]

From the perspective of 1840, John Reynolds, an Illinois Democrat, proclaimed:

> In the beginning, parties were organized on great and fundamental principles, and have continued down to the present time without change or alteration. The principles and policy that formed the basis of political action in the days of Jefferson are the *same* that govern the present Administration.[23]

Several years earlier, a Democratic colleague of Reynolds, Senator Thomas Morris, viewed Jackson's presidency, then just ending, as having represented a significant change in the direction of public policy, a veering away from the principles which comprised Clay's American System. Jackson's veto messages contained an old program for a new party, the Democracy.[24]

These historical oversimplifications contained a measure of perception and truth, especially those relating to the philosophy of government articulated by both Jefferson—mainly *before* he became president—and Jackson—largely *after* he became president. Jackson's presidency did indeed mark a rather basic change in emphasis in policy matters as well, though when specific actions are examined Jackson's concern

---

[18] (May 9, 1836) *ibid.* **3** (appendix): p. 337.
[19] (July 3, 1838) *ibid.* **6** (appendix): p. 458.
[20] (March 31, 1840) *ibid.* **8** (appendix): p. 323.

[21] (March 31, 1834) *ibid.* **1**: p. 281.
[22] (February 23, 1838) *ibid.* **6** (appendix): p. 167.
[23] (April 17, 1840) *ibid.* **8** (appendix): p. 340.
[24] (April (?), 1836) *ibid.* **3** (appendix): pp. 340–341.

for practical political considerations is also evident. But the larger point remains valid: though individual Democratic congressmen were occasionally perceptive in their understanding of basic political developments in the thirties, for the most part their analyses of the nature and history of parties were convenient over-simplifications, accepted without much thought, and designed to make the Democratic party and its predecessor appear as the people's party.

But what of the Whigs? The *Congressional Globe* does not contain similar comments from members of the emergent opposition. It was doubtless more difficult for the Whigs to find ready-made historical precedents within the context of American political life. Opposition to executive tyranny, which became the central tenet of the party in its formative years, suggested nothing more than Republican opposition to Federalist tyranny in the 1790's. And yet, Clay's legislative program was clearly based on the measures Hamilton advocated during the years of Washington's administrations. Perhaps mindful of this contradiction, Whigs who sought historic justification for their name conjured up a British frame of reference, with President Jackson as King Andrew I and with the new Whigs carrying on the age-old opposition to monarchical usurpation.

These scattered references from congressional debates illustrate the fact that a politician's identification with party carried over from nomination, campaign, and election into congressional activity to an increasing extent during the period of the formation of the second-party system. Congressmen did not necessarily like such a development; some continued throughout the decade to oppose it or at least to have qualms about it, though others eventually supported it publicly. What is equally evident about the politics of these years is that the extent to which issues became "party" issues varied considerably. Voting records adequately document this. But the *reasons* for it, though suggested by sporadic comments made during debates, are not as clear. Among the factors, already mentioned, which must be taken into account are: presidential pressure, the interests of constituents, the influence of the parties on candidates during campaigns and elections, and a complex web of relationships between a congressional delegation and its state's political life.

THE TARIFF

Of all the major issues of the thirties, the one least affected by the parties in Congress was the one largely "resolved" before Democrats and Whigs were organized everywhere in the country: the tariff. Congressional voting on the tariff bills of 1832 and 1833 does not reveal a pattern in any sense along party lines, even among representatives and senators from the Northeast, where party organizations had definitely

been established for the purpose of nominating and electing Jacksonians and their opponents. Jackson himself left to Congress what he called a "modification" of the tariff, whose rates he thought should be determined on the basis of making American industry competitive with foreign, something which should be done apart from party conflicts. In his first Annual Message to Congress the President articulated a policy which he did not deviate from in any significant way in subsequent messages:

> The general rule to be applied in graduating the duties upon articles of foreign growth or manufacture is that which will place our own in fair competition with those of other countries; and the inducements to advance even a step beyond this point are controlling in regard to those articles which are of primary necessity in time of war. When we reflect upon the difficulty and delicacy of this operation, it is important that it should never be attempted but with the utmost caution. . . .
> In deliberating, therefore, on these interesting subjects local feelings and prejudices should be merged in the patriotic determination to promote the great interests of the whole. All attempts to connect them with the party conflicts of the day are necessarily injurious, and should be discountenanced. Our action upon them should be under the control of higher and purer motives. . . . Discarding all calculations of political ascendancy, the North, the South, the East, and West should unite in diminishing any burthen of which either may justly complain.[25]

Jackson returned to the subject in his second Annual Message. He disagreed with those who argued that a "protective" tariff was unconstitutional:

> The power to impose duties on imports originally belonged to the several states. The right to adjust those duties with a view to the encouragement of domestic industries is so completely incidental to that power that it is difficult to suppose the existence of one without the other.

The President, having thus affirmed his belief that Congress had the power to control imports, even if it meant protecting domestic manufacturers, decried the tendency of some politicians to ascribe all the nation's economic problems to whatever happened to be the tariff schedule at the moment of their alarm. Jackson favored a modification of the rates, because "the present tariff taxes some of the comforts of life unnecessarily high; it undertakes to protect interests too local and minute to justify a general exaction, and it also attempts to force some kinds of manufacturing for which the country is not ripe." What the President feared most of all was an act "of majorities founded not on identity of conviction, but on combinations of small minorities entered into for the purpose of mutual assistance in measures which, resting solely on their own merits, could never have been carried." Therefore, it was of the utmost

---

[25] James D. Richardson, editor, *A Compilation of the Messages and Papers of the Presidents* (Washington, 1897) 3: p. 1013. Henceforth cited as Richardson, editor, *Messages and Papers*.

importance that congressmen legislate in the *national* interest, avoiding both purely local considerations and—again—"partisan conflicts." For, "to make this great question, which unhappily so much divides and excites the public mind, subservient to the short-sighted views of faction must destroy all hope of settling it satisfactorily to the great body of the people and for the general interest." Therefore, "objects of national importance alone ought to be protected." Once again the President urged careful deliberation: "I am well aware that this is a subject of so much delicacy, on account of the extended interests it involves, as to require that it should be touched with utmost caution. . . ." [26]

In his fourth Annual Message, presented on December 4, 1832, after the nullification crisis involving South Carolina had developed, but before compromise tariff proposals were introduced by both administration and opposition congressmen, Jackson modified his position:

Experience . . . makes it doubtful whether the advantages of this system are not counterbalanced by many evils, and whether it does not tend to beget in the minds of a large portion of our countrymen a spirit of discontent and jealousy dangerous to the stability of the Union. . . . Those who take an enlarged view of the condition of our country must be satisfied that the policy of protection must be ultimately limited to those articles of domestic manufacture which are indispensable to our safety in time of war. . . . That manufactures adequate to the supply of our domestic consumption would in the abstract be beneficial to our country there is no reason to doubt. [But, in view of the foregoing,] if upon investigation it shall be found . . . that the legislative protection granted to any particular interest is greater than is indispensably requisite for these objects, I recommend that it be gradually diminished, and that . . . the whole scheme of the duties be reduced to the revenue standard as soon as a just regard to the faith of the Government and to the preservation of the large capital invested in establishments of domestic industry will permit.[27]

These remarks clearly reveal Jackson's obvious bias *in favor of* a protective tariff system, one that would have been both rational and national. What is also obvious is his sensitivity to political realities. His emphasis on a "cautious" approach to congressional action, his repeated references to the "delicacy" of the subject, and his eventual modification—in the midst of the nullification crisis—of the views stated at the outset of his presidency, all indicate Jackson's reluctance to adhere rigidly to principle on an issue which was as divisive as protection was. From the beginning, though, he urged that the matter be acted upon apart from "partisan" or party politics. In this way only can Jackson be considered to have been consistent throughout his presidency. So, flat presidential opposition was one reason that the tariff never became a party issue. There were others. One was

that the emergent parties could not afford to adhere to a well-defined position on a matter which divided their rank-and-file from the beginning. Voting in 1832 and 1833 was clearly based upon local considerations that were too deeply engrained for any party leader to attempt to eradicate. Presidential hopes to the contrary, the very nature of a tariff bill—with its long lists of rates for products produced in many distinct areas of the country—guaranteed the primacy of local and not national concerns. Furthermore, the major pieces of tariff legislation from 1816 to 1828 had all been enacted during a period in which parties did not even exist as organized entities in Congress.

The crisis in federal-state relations between the national government and South Carolina produced a major shift in tariff policy as a result of the compromise supported by the administration and opposition leader Senator Henry Clay. When the "national interest" was finally in fact associated with tariff legislation, the former was given a moderate definition, something between the extremist positions held by those who favored a high, indiscriminate schedule and by those who opposed protection altogether—in short, the definition Jackson gave the national interest in his 1832 Message. But this was not the work of parties.

INTERNAL IMPROVEMENTS

President Jackson enunciated a well-defined policy on another matter, which was to be debated continuously throughout the decade. In his first Annual Message he urged that appropriations continue to be made for various internal improvements projects in the states, as "every member of the Union, in peace and in war, will be benefited by the improvement of inland navigation and the construction of highways in the several states." But, to avoid the controversy which had surrounded the introduction of such measures in the past, Jackson urged that the surplus revenue, to accumulate shortly when the national debt was extinguished, be distributed among the states according to their representation in Congress and that a constitutional amendment be enacted which would give Congress the power to do so.[28] Jackson repeated his request for such an amendment in his second Annual Message.[29]

In his veto of the Maysville and Lexington Road bill, the President added to his views on the subject. He opposed federal appropriations for local internal improvements projects, and, because there was so much uncertainty concerning the proper scope of power for the federal government, he again urged that there be a constitutional amendment clearly defining the power. Jackson thus repeated the position taken earlier by Jefferson, Madison, and Monroe during their presidencies. Indeed a large section of the veto

---

[26] *Ibid.*, pp. 1087–1088.
[27] *Ibid.*, pp. 1161–1162.

[28] Richardson, editor, *Messages and Papers* 3: p. 1015.
[29] *Ibid.*, p. 1077.

message is a summary of Madison's message of 1817 and Monroe's of 1822, and, except for slight changes in emphasis, Jackson's own contribution mirrors those of his predecessors.[30]

Subsequent bills of the same, local nature were also vetoed by the President, who simply referred Congress to his first veto message for the explanation.[31] The only exception was harbor and river improvements in areas where foreign commerce was centered:

It is indisputable that whatever gives facility and security to navigation cheapens imports, and all who consume them are alike interested in whatever produces this effect. . . . The consumer in the most inland state derives the same advantage that he does who resides in a maritime state.[32]

So, Jackson generally gave river and harbor bills of this kind his signature. In his sixth Annual Message, delivered in December, 1834, the President reviewed what he clearly thought had been his persistent efforts to block passage of internal improvement bills of a local character:

Nearly four years have elapsed, and several sessions of Congress have intervened, and no attempt within my recollection has been made to induce Congress to exercise this power [at least with respect to roads]. The applications for the construction of roads and canals which were formerly multiplied upon your files are no longer presented, and we have good reason to infer that the current of public sentiment has become so decided against the pretension as effectually to discourage its reassertion.[33]

The question of concern here is not what motivated Jackson, something which has vexed historians for a long time, but what, if anything, was the impact of the President's policy on the development of party politics in Congress? Unfortunately, the original vote on the Maysville Road bill is not tallied in the official record of the congressional debates, though that on passage over the veto is. A direct comparison between the two votes is not possible, but the shift is not large: 102–86 in favor of the original; 96–90 against the veto. At most Jackson's disapproval affected only a handful of representatives. An analysis of the second vote reveals that a significant number of Jacksonians from states whose people were concerned with internal improvement projects— Maryland, Pennsylvania, Kentucky, Ohio—simply would not support him, even to the point of voting to override the veto.[34]

Jackson's subsequent sporadic vetoes and occasional references to the subject in annual messages did not have any more effect. Though fewer in number than during the Adams' administration, internal improvements bills continued to be debated in Congress. And a bill to extend the national road was almost an annual occurrence.

In February, 1836, Democratic Senator James Buchanan of Pennsylvania neatly summarized the argument against internal improvements ever becoming either a national or a party issue:

If we had pursued the system of appropriating money for the construction of roads and canals all over the Union, the attention of Congress would thus have been diverted from the great objects entrusted to our care by the Constitution. Our time would have been almost exclusively occupied in this business. Besides, although each member might have prescribed it as a rule for himself to grant no appropriations except to national objects, yet when a road or canal was proposed affecting . . . the interests of his own constituents, he would have been ingenious in satisfying himself that it was of general importance. Such is the nature of man. Each member would have to decide this question for himself, and each decision would have been a precedent, upon the strength of which we might go a little further. The natural tendency of the system was to proceed to such an extent that, instead of legislating for the great interests of the Union, the chief objects of our pursuit would have been to obtain money from the Treasury to be expended upon roads and canals for the benefit of our constituents.[35]

On the same day, Democratic Senator John Tipton of Indiana, who favored the bill to extend the national road, told his colleagues that

he would regret to see the question on the passage of this bill made a party question; indeed he did not see how it could be made so. It had never been considered a party measure, and of the political parties that had existed in this country for the last 30 years, some members had supported and others have opposed appropriations for the national road, without regard to political bearing.[36]

In the 1838 version of the debate, by which time congressmen were fully aware of their party affiliation in a continuous, persuasive way, Joseph Underwood, a Whig representative from Kentucky who opposed additional funds for the road, said:

There is something *wonderful* in the amalgamating influences of the Cumberland road. It operates like magic. The Whigs of Ohio, Indiana, and Illinois walk as lovingly with their political adversaries on this particular question as if they had always, on all questions, been perfectly agreed! How happens it that even where this road touches the Old Dominion, it makes the representative a good internal improvement man, and seems to silence all the Constitutional scruples in voting money for that purpose? I dare say, when our constituents are getting money, and we, in consequence, are getting their votes, that all so situated have irreversible motives to support appropriations to continue this road.[37]

---

[30] *Ibid.*, pp. 1046–1056.

[31] Specifically, the Washington Turnpike Road bill (1830), the Louisville and Portland Canal bill (1830), "an act for the improvement of certain harbors and the navigation of certain rivers" (1832), and "an act to improve the navigation of the Wabash River" (1834), *ibid.*, pp. 1056–1057, 1071–1077, 1201–1202, 1337–1339.

[32] *Ibid.*, p. 1072.

[33] *Ibid.*, pp. 1339–1340. The often repeated charge that Jackson was flagrantly inconsistent in his internal improvement policies is thus clearly unwarranted.

[34] *Register of Debates* 6: pp. 842, 1147–1148.

[35] (February 26, 1836) *Congressional Globe* 3 (appendix): p. 165.

[36] (February 26, 1836) *ibid.* 3 (appendix): p. 159.

[37] (April 18, 1838) *ibid.* 6 (appendix): p. 521.

By 1840, a presidential election year and six years after the initial organization of the Whig and Democratic parties, party pressure on congressmen reached the highest intensity of the decade. Even internal improvements, which of all the continuously debated issues had been the least susceptible to such pressures, became at least a subject of discussion within the framework of party politics. And voting, at least on appropriations for the continuation of the national road, reflected this interest in that the division, though far from a simple Whig-Democratic split, revealed more Whigs in favor and more Democrats in opposition than ever before. Thirty-five out of the eighty-seven who voted affirmatively were Democrats. Thirty-one out of ninety who voted negatively were Whigs.[38]

It was in the interest of Westerners, especially those whose constituents would benefit directly, to argue that party politics should be entirely omitted from congressional action on this matter. As Whig representative Samson Mason of Ohio put it:

He, for one, disclaimed all intention, all purpose, of subjecting this measure to such an unhallowed test. The two great political parties of the country had not divided on this question, though gentlemen from each had taken different sides as to the expediency of progressing with the Cumberland road. Gentlemen of both parties had stood in opposition to the measure. . . . Therefore, the gentlemen of the West, of both parties, should act with some concert.[39]

Democratic Senator John Norvell of Michigan made explicit what many of his colleagues must have been thinking:

Another Presidential election was approaching; and always, on the eve of such an event, it was perhaps to be expected, that a few states, having interests in common, pursuing a common object, elated with the importance of their electoral votes to both parties, and aware of the anxiety of both to secure them, should combine to press, under circumstances so auspicious, a favorite measure to their section of the country.[40]

But some thought they detected the influence of party even in the West, where fully developed, competitive party organizations were of recent origins and, in a few instances, had not yet appeared.[41] J. Ogden Hoffman, Whig representative from New York, asserted that the national road issue had been decisive in the last Indiana congressional election, when five Democrats and three Whigs were victorious. The Democrats, at least, hoped for an appropriation so that Van Buren could win Indiana's electoral votes in the fall's presidential election. This charge evoked a sharp reaction from two of the Democratic representatives. Tilghman Howard denied the preemi-

nence Hoffman had given to the internal improvements issue:

I would say to him, that so far as one district of that state is concerned, his information is not well founded. . . . Rarely was the subject of the Cumberland road mentioned by either my opponent or myself. We discussed other topics: the Sub-Treasury; the United States Bank; the merits of the late and present Administrations, and especially the charges made against them of fraud, corruption, and extravagance. In seventy-five addresses which I delivered, these were the subjects I discussed. . . . I appeal, therefore, to gentlemen of all parties, in behalf of what I regard as the redemption of a pledge given for the construction of this great work. It is not party feeling that brings us here in regard to this road. In relation to it, we have but one party, one interest, one purpose.[42]

John W. Davis likewise denied that their position on the national road was the only reason representatives from districts through which the proposed road would pass were in Congress. In fact, some of the Democrats in the Indiana delegation were elected from districts quite separate from the route. Davis accused Hoffman of making internal improvements a party issue, in his own mind at least, by offering as the reason for his [Hoffman's] opposition alleged evidence that Democrats hoped to gain politically from an additional appropriation.[43]

Others, such as Representative Daniel Barnard, a Whig from New York, favored continued national support for internal-improvements projects, but could no longer keep the issue completely separate from party politics. Barnard admitted this by saying that

he had no disposition to connect this subject with party, but did not believe it was possible for him, more than others, to divorce it entirely from party. He hoped, however, whatever aspect it should assume with reference to party, it should be of national and patriotic cast, and be not merged into local and personal party contests. The question was one which commanded the favor of every President of the United States, every Administration of government, every party in power, and every party of any considerable standing which expected to get into power, since the system was first introduced.[44]

Even those opposed to further government support had to admit the growing influence of party. Senator John C. Calhoun asked his colleagues whether they could doubt

that there is, in reality, a large portion of this body discontented with so large an annual draft on the treasury for a single work, as local in its character as a thousand others that may be named? Nay, further; can we doubt that there is a great majority of the body of both parties opposed to it, both on the ground of expediency and Constitutionality, but who feel themselves compelled, in a measure, to vote for the appropriation, because of its supposed bearing on a certain question which now agitates the country [the coming election], but which he did not deem proper to name here.[45]

[38] *Ibid.* **8**: p. 415.
[39] (January 8, 1840) *ibid.* **8**: p. 175.
[40] (March 26, 1840) *ibid.* **8** (appendix): p. 296.
[41] McCormick, *The Second American Party System*, pp. 320–326. Indiana was one of the last states to develop in this sense.

[42] (February 12, 1840) *Congressional Globe* **8** (appendix): pp. 190, 192.
[43] (April 30, 1840) *ibid.* **8** (appendix): p. 444.
[44] (February 14, 1840) *ibid.* **8**: p. 199.
[45] (April 1, 1840) *ibid.* **8** (appendix): p. 369.

John Bell, long-time Whig representative from Tennessee, was not so delicate: "We are now on the eve of a Presidential election, and that is the cause why there is a more animated struggle upon the question of continuing these improvements." [46] President Van Buren became directly involved in the controversy by omitting the usual request for an appropriation to continue work on the national road because, the President argued, the Treasury simply did not have sufficient funds. Representative Richard Biddle, a Whig from Pennsylvania, accused the President of acting for "electioneering purposes." In Biddle's view, friends of the administration wanted Congress to appear odious and extravagant by increasing proposed expenditures, thus giving Van Buren the appearance of being a champion of economy and frugality, even though he had not been.[47]

Two Democrats responded to this charge. John Reynolds of Illinois, who supported an appropriation, scorned those who opposed the House bill just because it had not been suggested by the President. Van Buren had recommended such a measure in previous sessions, but now left it,

as it should be, to the free action of Congress. . . . We have heard much said in this hall against the dictation, and party discipline of the President, and that the Democrats were not free, but bound neck and heels by Executive shackles. . . . I dare any man to return to his constituents and tell them that he was not independent enough to support this measure, because the President did not recommend it.[48]

A few days later, John Jameson of Missouri added to Reynold's argument by accusing the Whigs of being grossly inconsistent. They claimed their cardinal principle was opposition to executive tyranny, yet they would not support a bill which the Van Buren administration did not first introduce, thereby abdicating congressional power. After all, the President had simply heeded the advice of Congress, which had refused to approve appropriations in the past. It was difficult for Jameson—at least—to escape the conclusion that the Whigs wanted, in an election year, to blame Van Buren for the road's not being built.[49] But Jameson's conclusion was not the only explanation. If Whigs generally did not in fact think of the road bill as a legitimate party measure, and thus one claiming their support, they could hardly be called inconsistent if they did not rally in support of an appropriation the President had neglected to offer.

In any case, the Whigs also accused the administration party of inconsistency, albeit of a different kind. Bell noted, on the basis of speeches he had heard in the House, "that in some portions of the country the Democracy opposed the measure; and in others,

sustained it." [50] This charge apparently forced Reynolds to make an exaggerated defense of the Democrats as the party which supported the bill, while the Whigs opposed it. In January his message had been quite different:

But on a subject of importance to the West that this was, he appealed to western gentlemen to discard politics and discuss it with reference to its merits alone. No political capital could be gained by either party from this measure, and he would put it to his western friends whether a measure they had so much at heart would not be injuriously affected by dragging it into the political arena.

I entreat . . . my western friends to join me in my endeavors to get the action of this House in favor of this measure, and laying politics aside, assist in obtaining an appropriation for it. This road was, strictly speaking, a national measure.[51]

But on April 17, after Bell had made his remarks, Reynolds pointed to such Whig leaders as Clay and Southard in the Senate, Hoffman and Bell in the House, as having led the opposition to the road continuation bill during the last session. The negative decision in both houses "was the result of the labored exertions of the most influential and talented gentlemen of the Whig party." [52] And though Reynolds was delighted to find that opposition members from Ohio, Indiana, and Illinois "did not join with their colleagues in the *death and murder* of the Cumberland road," he nevertheless held the Whig party responsible for the defeat of the measure. And yet his own breakdown of the Senate vote (Democrats 13–10 in favor; Whigs 7–12 opposed) revealed more than anything else a lack of party unity. His claim that a majority of those who voted affirmatively in the House were Democrats is simply not true. What Reynolds wanted was for all Westerners to support the bill at the same time he hoped Democrats elsewhere would support the measure on party grounds. Reynolds was, in fact, himself inconsistent, though in a way that not even the Whigs had thought of.

The importance of all this talk about the influence of party on voting is that politicians towards the end of the decade were so mindful of party pressures that some detected such pressures even where they had limited impact. Obviously, some congressmen voted for or against appropriations for the national road— especially in 1840—because of Van Buren's position on the matter. But those who were most vociferous on the subject of party influence tended to exaggerate for effect, to blame those who disagreed with them for allowing themselves to be subjected to it, or to urge everyone to rise above it, or even (in the case of Reynolds) to advocate unity for their own party at the same time that they lauded the independence of opposition members who sided with them. In these bizarre ways the issue which resisted party divisions

---

[46] (February 17, 1840) *ibid.* **8**: p. 207.
[47] (January 8, 1840) *ibid.* **8**: pp. 174–175.
[48] (April 17, 1840) *ibid.* **8** (appendix): pp. 343–344.
[49] (April 21, 1840) *ibid.* **8** (appendix): p. 454.

[50] (February 29, 1840) *ibid.* **8**: p. 230.
[51] (January 8, 1840) *ibid.* **8**: p. 175.
[52] (April 17, 1840) *ibid.* **8** (appendix): p. 343.

more than any other throughout the thirties finally succumbed.

INDIAN REMOVAL

Debate over the administration-approved Indian Removal bill assumed a "party" character to a surprisingly significant extent scarcely over a year after Jackson became President, however. The only significant defections in the House among those who had supported Jackson in the election of 1828 were in the Pennsylvania delegation, where thirteen out of twenty-two identifiable Jacksonians voted against the bill, and in the Ohio delegation, where five out of ten did the same. But they did not do so until after one of their number, Joseph Hemphill of Pennsylvania, had proposed an amendment requiring the President to appoint commissioners to survey the Indians for their opinion of the proposed removal to land granted them west of the Mississippi River. Not only would passage of the amendment result in the gathering of important information, but the resultant delay in removal was also desirable because "it appears ... that the people of this country are not prepared for this question; they have not yet had an opportunity to reflect upon it." Hemphill admitted that "...it is endeavored to place this important question on party grounds, but it is too important: it deeply involves both the political and moral character of the country." And, as if apologizing for the difference between himself and Jackson, he added: "The President has not more sincere friends in the United States than those of his party who prefer this amendment to the original bill, and I predict that they will be discovered to have been his most discreet friends on this occasion." [53]

Hemphill's amendment was defeated, but by the slimmest of margins, 99–98, with Speaker Andrew Stevenson's vote deciding the matter. On the final vote four Jacksonians who had earlier supported Hemphill, decided to express their approval of the original bill and bolstered the majority for it to 102–97. [54]

Light on the other major defection, that within the Ohio delegation, was cast a few days later during a House debate over the President's veto of the Maysville Road bill. William Stanberry, elected as a supporter of Jackson, revealed why he, and perhaps others in the Ohio delegation, opposed the Indian Removal bill. He felt many had voted for the measure against their consciences, "in consequence of their not having the independence to resist what they supposed to be the wishes of the executive. They were literally dragooned into its support." According to Stanberry, further evidence of this alleged incidence of party pressure was that opponents of federal aid to

internal improvements projects supported the Indian Removal bill with the understanding that appropriations would then be denied to such projects. He added, "We, who are friends of this Administration," were denounced by self-appointed Jacksonian leaders from the President's home-state of Tennessee, which was the basis for their exalted position in the Government. [55]

This was too much for James K. Polk, of the group just referred to. Rising with the comment he was glad Stanberry had thrown off his political mask, Polk went on to assert the Ohioan had been elected as a friend of Jackson, but had not supported a single measure favored by the administration during the current session. Polk wondered aloud whether Stanberry had used Jackson's popularity to get elected. In any case, "the member had formed new associations recently—associations with our old political adversaries; and he was glad, for the future, to know who he was, and where to find him." [56] What Polk did not add was that Stanberry's political behaviour should also be viewed within the context of a state whose political system, while quite well organized by the presidential election of 1828, was newly emergent, the kind of system in which fluctuating allegiances and not loyalty or consistency was perhaps the most obvious characteristic. [57]

John Bell, another Tennesseean, was also upset by Stanberry's remarks. Repeating what Polk had said, Bell moved on to deny there had been "party action" on the removal bill, which he thought had passed without the approval of many Jacksonians, and, indeed, "had a closing reply been permitted I was prepared to disavow any interest on the part of friends of the Administration in the measure, as a party measure, and to let the responsibility of its passage or rejection rest wholly with those who doubted its policy, or opposed it on party grounds." If only the popularity of the Jackson administration were involved, the bill deserved to be defeated. He and others had been indifferent to the outcome if the bill were to be treated as a party measure. To be sure, opposition members claimed it was an electioneering scheme, "but the Indian question rose above the party conflicts of the day." [58]

But did it? An examination of the vote reveals a division whose relationship to party was fairly obvious. Though thirty-two out of the ninety-seven (about one-third) who opposed the bill were identifiable Jacksonians, eighteen of that number were from Pennsylvania and Ohio. Excluding these two states only New York (3), Virginia (2), and North Carolina (2) provided more than one negative vote. Many, especially from Ohio, New York, and Virginia, rejected

[53] (May 24, 1830) *Register of Debates* 6: p. 1132.
[54] (May 24, 1830) *ibid.* 6: pp. 1133, 1135.

[55] (May 28, 1830) *ibid.* 6: pp. 1139–1140.
[56] (May 28, 1830) *ibid.* 6: pp. 1140–1142.
[57] McCormick, *The Second American Party System*, pp. 263–265.
[58] (May 28, 1830) *Register of Debates* 6: pp. 1145–1146.

the administration position on *both* the removal bill and the road bill, which was the obverse of Stanberry's charge that there was evidence of a deal involving those who supported Jackson on the removal bill and who later approved of his veto of the road bill.

And there is also evidence that opposition members in the House were aware of the role party played with respect to the removal issue. William Storrs of Connecticut, though not identified by the congressional directory as an Adams supporter, said: "I have been a party man..., perhaps too much so—and I have contributed nothing to place the present chief magistrate in the station which he now holds—as yet under the Constitution and not over it," and went on to vote against removal on the grounds that representatives ought to consult further with their constituents about the question.[59] John Test, a Clay supporter from Indiana, told his colleagues in the House he would not support the measure, even though all the other members of his state's delegation favored it. Not even the state legislature's instructions to senators and request to representatives to support removal would sway him.[60]

In the Senate, party identification is much more difficult to determine for the early years of Jackson's presidency, simply because only one-third of that body was elected in 1828–1829, thus associating themselves either with or against Jackson's candidacy. Still, it is of significance and particularly relevant that not one senator in this limited group elected as a supporter of Jackson voted against removal and not one elected as an opponent voted in favor of it.[61]

There can be no doubt that the new President wanted congressional approval. Of all the matters discussed in his first Annual Message, the removal of the Indian tribes was the only one which took the form of a specific proposal:

[Since] the Constitution declares that "no new State shall be formed or erected within the jurisdiction of any other State" without the consent of its legislature . . . [the] portion . . . of the Southern tribes, having mingled much with the whites and made progress in the arts of civilized life . . . and lately attempted to erect an independent government within the limits of Georgia and Alabama [must not be permitted to do so.] [Congress should consider] setting apart an ample district west of the Mississippi, and without the limits of any State or Territory now formed. . . . This emigration should be voluntary. . . . But they should be distinctly informed that if they remain within the limits of the States they must be subject to their laws.[62]

The conclusion seems inescapable: On the very first issue in which Jackson took a personal interest, he was able to maintain the loyalty of a sizable majority of those congressmen who had been his supporters in the campaign of 1828. The remarks quoted above made by Stanberry, Polk, Bell, Storrs, and Test reveal that for the first time in fifteen years some politicians were aware of a new factor in congressional politics: the identification of party membership with positions taken on matters being considered. And though those who talked about the role of party did so in a faltering, often inaccurate, sometimes calculatingly contradictory way, they unmistakably revealed the awareness their colleagues had begun to have of party allegiance extending beyond campaigns and elections into the deliberations of Congress itself.

Though most who were opposed to Jackson's candidacy also voted together—against removal—it would be inaccurate to argue that this action represented the beginnings of a unified, continuous opposition party in Congress. Later on, at the opening of the next session of Congress, Clay wrote to a friend that "parties have not yet exhibited their respective strength; nor, except [for] the election of Speaker, has there been any occasion for its display. In that instance, there was evidently no concert between those opposed to the Administration; and such a concert I apprehend to be extremely difficult, if not impossible. . . ."[63] This, just weeks before the introduction of the bill to recharter the Bank of the United States. In this statement, Clay cryptically reveals both the existence of parties in Congress and their lack of continuity or even organization.

SLAVERY

Slavery became a subject of congressional concern in the middle of the decade when abolitionists, feminists, and others who were in some way hostile toward the South's "peculiar institution" joined together to petition Congress to abolish slavery in the nation's capital. From 1835 to 1840 hundreds of petitions were received by senators and representatives from Northern states, the result of what was obviously an organized effort.

A prolonged controversy over these antislavery petitions began one year after Congress had divided into parties on a nearly nation-wide basis, over the banking issue.[64] The question was, would party loyalty, so evident when Congress debated banking proposals, be a major determinant in voting on other important issues.

In the previous decade, the Missouri crisis linked the slavery issue with sectional division, both in and out of Congress. But that happened in a one-party era, and moderate Republicans from both North and South—especially after the depth of sectional antagonism had been revealed in debate by some of their

---

[59] (May 15, 1830) *ibid.* **6**: pp. 1014–1015.
[60] (May 19, 1830) *ibid.* **6**: p. 1103.
[61] (May 24, 1830) *ibid.* **6**: p. 1133.
[62] Richardson, editor, *Messages and Papers* **3**: 1021–1022.

[63] (December 9, 1831) Clay to Francis Brooke, Calvin Colton, editor, *The Private Correspondence of Henry Clay* (New York, 1855), p. 321. Henceforth cited as *Clay Correspondence.*
[64] The exception involved those congressmen from the most recently settled Western states.

more radical colleagues—worked hard for an acceptable compromise. Throughout the renewed debates of the thirties, many congressmen expressed a common fear that the issue would again lead to a flaring up of North-South animosity.

Such fears existed in a rather changed political context, however, something which was largely the result of the resuscitation of party. From its very beginning, the Jacksonian Democratic party had been dedicated to the proposition that the only way to construct a durable political movement with popular strength in both North and South was to remain silent about slavery. Certainly this was what Van Buren had in mind when he constructed much of the initial coalition which coalesced around the candidacy of Andrew Jackson in the late 1820's.[65]

1835–1836

As President, Jackson was silent, except for the recommendation contained in his Annual Message of December, 1835, that Congress pass "such a law as will prohibit, under severe penalties, the circulation in the Southern states, through the mail, of incendiary publications intended to instigate the slaves to insurrection,"[66] which was one way of insuring that everyone else remained silent as well. The President was responding to a request from a Southern postmaster for instructions on what to do with propaganda which abolitionist groups were sending South, where numerous meetings produced resolutions recommending the censorship of such writing. Though his proposal was defeated, Jackson had clearly gone on record in opposition to any public "agitation" of the subject of slavery.[67]

In Congress itself, the ensuing flood of "memorials" and resolutions favoring abolition in the District of Columbia produced a debate which focused on the right of petition versus the undesirability of congressional action on any aspect of the subject of slavery. But even more basic was the question: Should Congress debate the matter if such discussion could result in popular agitation threatening the very existence of the Union? After all, abolition could become "political" only if the major parties associated themselves in any way with the abolitionist position, for it was clear from the outset that the anti-slavery

leaders had no desire to form a party of their own. Thus, the major parties in Congress could remain united within themselves only if they opposed interference with slavery in any form. If they did not adopt such a position, the sectional antagonism of the twenties could reappear. Simply because of the potential sectional character of the slavery issue, the only possible position for a *united* party to take was a negative one.

Northern Democrats, at least, understood this. Representative Mann of New York indicated what must have been commonly understood by Jacksonians, especially in Van Buren's home state, for years:

The Union and Constitution . . . were the result of concession and compromise. The subject under debate formed one of the points.
We agreed—we entered into the compact with our Southern brethren; and the question now presented by them to us—the real question (when the argument is pushed to the full extent) propounded to us of the North, is whether we will live up to the bargain we have made to the compact and union we have entered into? For myself, for my constituents and friends, I answer without hesitation or mental reservation, that under all circumstances and in every vicissitude, good or evil, we will—we will, though the heavens fall.[68]

Representative Jarvis of Maine added that "his constituents deprecated the agitation of the question. They consider that it belongs exclusively to the Southern states, and that any interference by us would be unwise and unwarrantable." He referred to meetings held in Maine in which "party spirit was lost sight of" and resolutions adopted reproaching the abolitionists.[69]

In the Senate, Tallmadge of New York made the same point:

[Public meetings were held all over the state denouncing attempts] to disturb the peace of the Union. These meetings were held without distinction of party. Political dissensions were hushed, in the universal wish to put down this ill-judged and ill-timed agitation. . . . Friends of the Administration vied with each other in reprobating these incendiary efforts; . . . When you see presses that express the views of the great political parties into which the people of the state are divided, uniting on this subject, and representing the feelings of the great mass of the people throughout the state, can it be doubted that public sentiment of the people is sound?[70]

Democratic stalwart Isaac Hill, of New Hampshire underscored what Mann had said in the House:

I have said the people of the North were more united in their opposition to the plans of the advocates of anti-slavery, than on any other subject—this opposition is confined to no political party; it pervades every class of community. They depreciate all interference with the subject of slavery, because they believe such interference may involve the existence and welfare of the Union itself,

---

[65] Richard H. Brown, "The Missouri Crisis, Slavery, and the Politics of Jacksonianism," *South Atlantic Quart.* 65 (Winter, 1966): pp. 55–72.

[66] Richardson, *Messages and Papers* 3: p. 176.

[67] Both parties divided on the bill, and voting was not wholly along sectional lines either. (June 9, 1836) *Congressional Globe* 3: p. 430. The problem was resolved when postmasters were given authority to send such literature only to the few people in the South who actually subscribed to it, something Jackson had suggested earlier in a letter to Postmaster General Kendall. (August 7, 1835) Jackson to Amos Kendall, John S. Bassett, editor, *The Correspondence of Andrew Jackson* (7 v., Washington, 1926–1933) 5: p. 360. Henceforth cited as *Jackson Correspondence*.

[68] (December 22, 1835) *Congressional Globe* 3: p. 46.

[69] (January 6, 1836) *ibid.* 3: p. 75.

[70] (February 15, 1836) *ibid.* 3 (appendix): p. 111.

and because they understand the obligations which the non-slaveholding states owe to the slaveholding states by the compact of confederation. It is the strong desire to perpetuate the union . . . that now impels the united North to take its stand against the agitators of the anti-slavery project.[71]

Even the Democratic chairman of the House select committee on abolition in the District of Columbia, Pinckney of South Carolina, emphasized "he had nothing to do with party in reference to slavery, and therefore would not say anything that might have the remotest tendency to excite any party feeling on the subject."[72]

And yet, to those who wished for various reasons to find a scapegoat for the petitions controversy, the existence of parties in Congress was too fresh and important to ignore. Representative Pickens of South Carolina, spokesman for the small "state rights" party in the South, was outraged when he was accused of discussing the abolitionist threat "for party purposes," with the implication that "we desired some sectional excitement to raise us from our weak position, etc." Pickens would have ignored the remark "if it were not that it is understood to represent the executive branch of this government, that it is in the organ [the *Washington Globe*] of the dominant party that now rules the destinies of this republic." Pickens refused to remain silent on an issue that could split the Union. But he did not speak "to make it a question for partisan warfare or party triumph. It rises above all parties, and is identified with the dearest and paramount interests of every Southern state in this Confederacy."[73]

In the Senate, Preston of South Carolina gave the state rightists' explanation of the terrifying danger the abolitionists posed. In the closely divided states of the North, the major parties, "animated by the utmost intenseness of party spirit, . . . will be willing to snatch such arms as fury may supply, and avail themselves of such auxiliaries as chance may offer." The abolitionists, he argued, would remain neutral. Each of the major parties, apprehensive about an abolitionist alliance with the other party, would then woo the abolitionists' support. With their position thus enhanced, the abolitionists would then go on to absorb one or the other of the major parties. "The very fact of the reluctance which we all feel to agitate this matter here, bespeaks our fears of exasperating the strength which we instinctively know resides in the Abolitionists."[74] Calhoun put

the point more forcefully: Whatever position the major parties would take in the event of a sectional split over the slavery question, one or the other would certainly be considered favorable to the abolitionists' cause. The only way to prevent such a development was for *both* of the major parties to be united against abolition in any form whatsoever.[75]

This insistence upon total, uncompromising opposition to anything which could be interpreted as anti-slavery upset loyal Democrats who felt uneasy about their party's lack of complete unity. And though Calhoun and Preston had considerable insight into the future course of the anti-slavery, if not precisely abolitionist, movement as a political phenomenon, their comments about party produced responses from their erstwhile Democratic colleagues which seriously questioned the motivation of this little band of extremists. Democratic Senator Niles of Connecticut, accused the *Washington Telegram* and other press organs which supported the state rightist group with seeking to build up a sectional party through an appeal to the fears of Southerners by misrepresenting the essentially anti-abolitionist sentiment of Northerners. A Southern sectional party, he argued, would be a greater danger to the Union than a rather minor abolitionist movement.[76] Senator Brown of North Carolina was upset by Preston's charge that Democrats "had introduced topics of a party and political character into this debate." He hurled the charge back on the state rightists when he said "he well knew the untiring efforts which partisan politicians, and editors of newspapers of a certain political cast, were making to connect this question with party politics." There was no motive or inducement for regular Democrats to connect party politics with the slavery question. "On the contrary, *it was that very connection*, which himself and his friends had constantly deprecated as being fraught with the most pernicious consequence to the whole country."[77]

Representative Bynum of North Carolina spoke for his Democratic colleagues in the House when

he wished to know the facts, in justification of the party with which he acted, and to have it demonstrated whether the Abolition petitioners belonged to the Democratic Party, or to the other parties which acted in opposition to it. Mr. B. believed four-fifths or five-sixths of the

---

[71] (February 12, 1836) *ibid*. **3** (appendix): p. 91.

[72] (May 19, 1836) *ibid*. **3**: p. 386.

[73] (January 21, 1836) *ibid*. **3** (appendix): pp. 287–288. The *Globe* editorials on this subject reflected Jackson's concern that the state rightists, under Calhoun's leadership, would try to create a new Southern sectional party over the slavery issue. (April 9, 1833) Jackson to John Coffee, *Jackson Correspondence* **5**: p. 56.

[74] (March 1, 1836) *Congressional Globe* **3** (appendix): p. 222.

[75] (March 9, 1836) *ibid*. **3** (appendix): p. 226.

[76] (February 15, 1836) *ibid*. **3** (appendix): p. 118.

[77] (March 7, 1836) *ibid*. **3** (appendix): p. 271. Nearly three years earlier, at the end of the nullification controversy, Jackson himself predicted what his Democratic supporters were now concerned about. In April, 1833, he wrote to a friend: "Nullification is dead, but the Nullifiers in the South intend to blow up a storm on the subject of the slave question. Altho they know the East have no such views, still they will try to arouse the Southern people on the false tale. This ought to be met, for be assured, these men would do any act to destroy the Union, and form a Southern confederacy bounded, North, by the Patomac River. . . . " (April 9, 1833) Jackson to John Coffee, *Jackson Correspondence* **5**: p. 56.

Abolition petitions had come from individuals opposed to the Democratic party. Yet they were charged, day after day, . . . with aiding in keeping up the excitement and with deserting the interests of the South.[78]

As a Southern man, Bynum would defend Southern rights to the fullest extent, but he protested "on behalf of the party with whom he acted against the policy of self-appointed defenders of Southern interests."[79]

Bynum's remarks reveal how sensitive Democrats were to the charge that they tolerated abolitionist sympathizers. Even though the slavery issue was supposed to be far "above" party considerations as far as Democrats were concerned, anything less than party unanimity worried Southerners who feared the growth of a purely sectional party led by state rightists like Pickens and Calhoun. The Jacksonians were, in reality, thus ambivalent about the relationship between party loyalty and agitation over the South's peculiar institution.

Not so the Whigs. From the beginning it was apparent the opposition party would not be able to maintain a common position on the petitions controversy. Indeed, the range of opinion was immense. Senator Hoar of Massachusetts argued that Congress had the right to abolish slavery in the District of Columbia, while Senator Leigh of Virginia contended that Congress could not legislate on the subject of slavery at all. Leigh's explanation of such a wide spectrum of views was simple and frank: "Both gentlemen belong to a party that can disagree whenever and wherever it may be necessary."[80] Practically from their birth as a party, then, the Whigs agreed to disagree on that most divisive of issues, the only issue which could split a party along sectional lines.

So when Southern Whigs such as Representative Thompson of South Carolina loudly denounced allegations that the Whigs had got up "this discussion for party purposes," they could do so in complete honesty. It would have been political suicide for these politicans to leave the slightest ambiguity in the minds of their constituents about the existence of a "Whig" position on slavery at the very time their Northern colleagues favored the reception of anti-slavery petitions. Thompson's words thus have genuine emotion in them:

Those with whom I act here, sir, and with whom I have acted in times which are past, and in a crisis, everything of which I am willing should be forgotten, but the great principles which were asserted, a band of patriots whose party name is the only epitaph I wish upon my tomb, have been charged with getting up this discussion for party purposes. It is untrue. No Sir, we not only will not ourselves, nor will we allow others to touch this vital and delicate question for any such purpose. On this subject, hands off, is the word. Thus far you may go, but no farther. Let gentlemen here and elsewhere go on in their petty intrigues, their degrading scramble for offices, the honors of this Government. But there is one interest which will not be involved, and it is this.[81]

The House committee on abolition in the District of Columbia, which Speaker Polk stacked with all but one Democrats, reported on May 18, 1836, that (1) Congress had no authority to interfere in any way with slavery in the states; (2) that Congress "ought not to interfere in any way with slavery in the District of Columbia"; (3) that all petitions relating to the subject of slavery "shall, without being either printed or referred, be laid upon the table, and that no further action whatever shall be had thereon."[82] The vote on the first resolution was overwhelmingly affirmative: 182–9. All of the nine in opposition were Northern Whigs. On the second resolution, only eight Northern Democrats joined thirty-three Whigs to oppose the 132 representatives who favored inaction on slavery in Washington. The final resolution, the so-called "gag" rule, produced a somewhat closer division: 117–68, with twenty-one Democrats allying with forty-six Northern Whigs and a lone Southern Whig. Of the twenty-one Democrats six were disgruntled Southerners who had refused to vote on the first resolution, arguing the committee had exceeded its authority by even mentioning the subject of slavery in the states. Presumably their votes against the gag rule constituted further protest, something which brought the support of Robertson of Virginia, the lone Southern Whig renegade.[83]

Only four Northern Democrats in the House voted against both the second and third resolutions. The fifteen who voted against the gag were scattered through congressional delegations of many of the Northern states. Only in Ohio (three out of eight), Indiana (two out of six), New Jersey (three out of six), and Connecticut (two out of six) was there anything approaching a major defection.[84] During the next session of Congress the Senate also agreed to table anti-slavery petitions, by a vote of thirty-one to thirteen. Five Northern Democrats—Knight of Rhode Island, Niles of Connecticut, Wall of New Jersey, Morris of Ohio, and Tipton of Indiana—voted against the resolution.[85] Most of these "renegade" Democrats in both houses remained in office for at least the next Congress, which indicates that there was no attempt by the party organization to "purge"

---

[78] (May 19, 1836) *Congressional Globe* 3: p. 387.
[79] *Ibid.*
[80] (February 12, 1836) *ibid.* 3 (appendix): p. 93.

[81] (December 21, 1835) *ibid.* 3 (appendix): p. 15.
[82] (February 10 and May 18, 1836) *ibid.* 3: pp. 161, 383.
[83] (February 9, 1836) *ibid.* 3: p. 158.
[84] (May 26, 1836) *ibid.* 3: p. 406. Representative Borden, the lone Democrat in Massachusetts' congressional delegation, went along with his Whig colleagues. But when he switched to the Whig party as a candidate for reelection in 1836, he was defeated! Pearce, Rhode Island's Democratic representative, voted with his Whig colleague, but was defeated when he sought reelection. In New York's huge thirty-one-man Democratic House delegation, only one voted against the gag, and of Pennsylvania's fifteen Democrats only two did.
[85] (February 6, 1837) *ibid.* 4: p. 159.

those who disagreed with the majority view; indeed, continuance in office suggests the adoption of a position necessary for political survival in certain Northern districts.

1836–1838

And so, the first congressional debate over anti-slavery petitions produced the confusing situation of Democrats decrying attempts to make slavery a party issue while at the same time coming fairly close to achieving party unity in favor of shutting off debate. Ordinarily the Whigs would not have resisted the temptation to publicize this inconsistency. But they were so divided among themselves on the slavery issue, that they were never able to agree upon any overall, long-term political strategy.

Indeed, Whig disunity extended to the selection of regional candidates for the presidency in 1836 and, of course, the absence of a clear position on slavery during the campaign. But Van Buren as the Democratic candidate was, again not surprisingly, consistent in his opposition to any abolitionist scheme. In his inaugural he referred to the position he had taken during the campaign and indicated what his position as president would be:

I then declared that if the desire of those of my countrymen who were favorable to my election was gratified, "I must go into the Presidential chair the inflexible and uncompromising opponent of every attempt on the part of Congress to abolish slavery in the District of Columbia against the wishes of the slaveholding states, and also with a determination equally decided to resist the slightest interference with it in the states where it exists." I submitted also to my fellow-citizens, with fullness and frankness, the reasons which led me to this determination. The result authorizes me to believe that they have been approved and are confided in by a majority of the people of the United States, including those whom they most immediately affect. It now remains to add that no bill conflicting with these views can ever receive my Constitutional sanction.[86]

Democrats thus had guidance from their new party leader from the outset of his presidency. But guidance for Democrats and Whigs alike came from outside Washington as well. The presidential pronouncement was followed during the next four years by an increasing number of resolutions from state legislatures, some anti-slavery, some pro-slavery in character. During the 1837–1838 session, the Vermont legislature resolved that Congress had the right to abolish slavery in the District and urged its congressional delegation to work toward that end.[87] But Democratic Senator Hubbard of neighboring New Hampshire presented resolutions from that state's legislature recommending that slavery in the District be let alone unless the inhabitants wanted it abolished, resolutions which accurately reflected sentiment in

New Hampshire and coincided with Senator Hubbard's own views.[88] These two sets of resolutions neatly summarized much of the range of congressional opinion and were as distinctive and as far apart as New Hampshire and Vermont were in their political complexion.

The most important development of the session, however, was the reconciliation of the state-rights group in the South with the regular Democratic party. Calhoun indicated the shift when he accused the Whigs of having a "consolidationist" political creed which offered no Constitutional protection from abolitionists' attacks, a creed which indeed, encouraged them.[89] The state-rights leader then introduced a series of resolutions to test the opinion of the Senate on the slavery issue. Senator Buchanan of Pennsylvania frankly admitted that Calhoun's resolutions were a platform on which friends of the South in the North could stand and defend themselves from the abolitionists. The South's Northern friends would have gone farther on their own to defend Southern interests, he added, but feared a reaction in public opinion throughout the North. Always sensitive about Southern interests, Calhoun thought Buchanan supported his resolutions out of pity for the South, something Buchanan quickly denied.[90]

Ironically, only Senator McKean, Buchanan's Democratic colleague in Pennsylvania, consistently opposed Calhoun's resolutions as they came to a vote. Apparently McKean did so because he had presented his own, briefer set of resolutions which the Senate had ignored.[91] Of the Northern Democratic Senators only the generally independent-minded Knight of Rhode Island joined McKean in opposition to the resolution that it was inexpedient to abolish slavery in territories where it existed when the people in them had not asked for abolition (which was an early version of popular sovereignty). The two were also alone in their opposition to another of Calhoun's resolutions: that Congress should not interfere with slavery in the District because such action would violate the spirit with which Maryland and Virginia ceded the land in the first place. McKean got a new partner—Morris of Ohio—when he opposed the resolution calling systematic attacks on the institution of slavery a "breach of faith" with the slave states. Opposition increased when McKean and Morris were joined by Ruggles of Maine and Tipton of Indiana to record a negative vote on the resolution which declared that it was a duty of the government to resist moves to interfere with slavery.[92] But generally

---

[86] Richardson, *Messages and Papers* 4: p. 1535.
[87] (December 18, 1837) *Congressional Globe* 6: pp. 33–34.
[88] (December 18, 1837) *ibid.* 6: p. 36.
[89] (January 6, 1838) *ibid.* 6 (appendix): p. 37.
[90] (January 11, 1838) *ibid.* 6 (appendix): p. 73.
[91] (January 5, 1838) *ibid.* 6: p. 80. There were just two: (1) Congress could not abolish slavery in the states and (2) It was inexpedient to legislate on the subject in the District of Columbia.
[92] *Ibid.* 6: pp. 81, 96, 99 and 6 (appendix): pp. 53, 74.

Calhoun had correctly sensed the mood of the party he was rejoining in the Senate. Northern Democratic opposition to pro-slavery positions all but disappeared when the Southern extremist forced the party he was returning to to go on record.

Southern Whigs assumed the role played by Democrats in the previous Congress of chastising the state-rights group with trying to create the impression it was the only party in the South opposed to the abolitionists. As Senator Crittenden of Kentucky put it:

What is this but saying to the Abolitionists "Go on, Go on; all is in your favor, do not calculate on any opposition but from me and the state rights party. . . . What! Are there no friends to the South but the gentleman and his little party? Is it left so weak, so helpless, so friendless, as to have no friends, no sympathy, no supporters in the whole country, but the gentleman himself and his little state rights party?"[93]

Calhoun's response was that the state-rights party, at least, had a political creed to counter the abolitionists. Since he and his colleagues believed that the United States was a federal republic comprised of states and not a consolidated republic made up of the mass of people in the aggregate, governmental action involving abolition would not be permitted if their views prevailed. He inferred that the Whigs adhered to the "consolidationist" view of governmental power and could therefore not be trusted on the slavery question.[94]

The Democrats also assumed a new role in this session, one that the state-rights group had played earlier to the accompaniment of vociferous denunciations from the Democrats themselves. Senator Pierce of New Hampshire repeated the warning originally made by Calhoun, Preston, and Pickens that the abolitionists were injecting the slavery issue into party politics at election time in various Northern states. In most cases only one party supported abolitionists' petitions, but in at least one state, Connecticut, he claimed *both* were. Pierce used this evidence to support his position that all politicians should rise above partisan considerations and remove from political life this most vexing of issues—"the only question that *can* lead to a dissolution of this Union."[95]

The House voted to reimpose the gag rule at the outset of the 1837–1838 session by a vote of 122–74. Twenty Northern Democrats joined fifty-four Whigs in opposition, five *more* renegades than in the last session. Of that seventeen, seven were from the Ohio delegation (all but one of the Democrats in that state's delegation), and three of those seven are recorded as having presented anti-slavery petitions to the House. Also among that number were half (three) of Connecticut's six-man, solidly Democratic delegation (two of whom presented anti-slavery

petitions), and all three of Massachusetts' Democratic representatives (one of whom presented such petitions), as well as Vermont's lone Democrat (who also presented petitions).[96] As was the case earlier, most of these Democrats remained in office for the next Congress. And, although a number of them did so, not even the presentation of anti-slavery memorials was a necessary prelude to an "anti-party" position in the voting on the gag.

1838–1839

During the following session there were indications of increasing strain during the continuing debates over what to do with the never ending stream of anti-slavery petitions. On several occasions House Speaker Polk ruled members out of order when they tried to speak frankly about the political ramifications and problems which the petitions controversy had led to. Representative Wise, Democrat of Virginia, was so disturbed when he interpreted House rulings on tabling to mean that the House had in fact actually "received" petitions that he "desired the clerk to note the fact that he had refused to vote, and he further desired him henceforth never to call his name on any vote on the subject of abolition."[97] If reception, "viz.: to recognize the jurisdiction of Congress over the subject of slavery, except directly in the slaveholding states," was all the South had gained from the Democrats, "a Northern party with Southern principles; . . . [then] it is a compact nothing better than Abolition itself."[98]

Whig Representative Biddle of Pennsylvania did not vote on a resolution that petitions regarding slavery in the District were part of a plan indirectly to destroy slavery, a resolution which he thought falsely stigmatized the mass of petitioners:

Whilst he could not vote for it, he knew the reckless audacity with which a vote against it might be used to create a false impression. Mr. B referred to the stand he had taken in his own district on this subject, and the manner in which he had been sustained. His Van Buren opponent had refused to answer the interrogatories propounded. Mr. B thought that a body of honorable men ought not to place him in this false light for the mere transient purposes of party, with a view to influence the elections at the South, now that those at the North had been got through with it. Mr. B was proceeding further, but

The chair interposed, on the grounds that the gentleman was transgressing the rules.

The House refused to excuse Mr. Biddle.[99]

[93] (January 9, 1838) *ibid*. 6 (appendix): p. 55.
[94] (January 9, 1838) *ibid*. 6 (appendix): p. 57.
[95] (January 9, 1838) *ibid*. 6 (appendix): p. 55.

[96] (December 21, 1837) *ibid*. 6: p. 45. Vermont's Democrat was probably influenced by his state legislature's anti-slavery resolutions. In states with sizable Democratic contingents in their congressional delegations, only two out of twenty-nine Democrats from New York voted against the gag, just two out of seventeen from Pennsylvania, and one out of six from Maine. Only one Southern Whig voted with these Democrats, and he did so for unknown reasons.
[97] (December 20, 1838) *ibid*. 7: p. 56.
[98] (December 14, 1838) *ibid*. 7: p. 34.
[99] (December 12, 1838) *ibid*. 7: p. 27.

The petition Biddle referred to was one of a series which Representative Atherton, a Democrat from New Hampshire, introduced at the beginning of the session.   Calhoun's Senate resolutions of the previous session were their obvious model, and like Calhoun's, Atherton's proposals were designed to put the House on record respecting its opinions on slavery.   The key test was on the reimposition of the gag rule.   Fifteen Northern Democrats (five fewer than in the previous session) joined fifty-seven Whigs in opposition.   The only significant defection was in New York, where five out the state's twenty-nine Democrats turned against the position which Van Buren so obviously favored.   None of these five returned to the next Congress—either because of defeat or resignation— which suggests a kind of "purge," though the very high rate of the turnover in the New York delegation in the 1830's keeps this from being a firm conclusion. All three of Massachusetts' Democrats continued to vote with their Whig colleagues.   And two of Connecticut's solidly Democratic delegation also voted against the gag.   But nowhere else in the North was there more than a lone Democratic renegade.   The other resolutions, with the exception of a few innocuous ones, were passed by lopsided majorities, with the number of Northern Democratic opponents reduced to handfuls.   As in the Senate, when the Democrats were forced to declare themselves publicly on pro-slavery propositions few wanted to vote against them.[100]   Only on the gag rule was a significant number of Northern adherents willing to break party unity.

Later in the session, one of the "loyal" Democrats from New York launched into the most forthright speech given to that time on the growing relationship Democrats saw between the Whigs and the abolitionists.   Indeed, he was so forthright that the House reporter added:

Note: Mr. Moore was called to order, in the course of his remarks, by General Waddy Thompson [Whig of South Carolina], and by the decision of the chair was prevented from concluding his speech.   Mr. Moore, before taking his seat, gave notice that he would publish all that he had intended to say, precisely in the same form and manner he would have done had no interruption taken place.[101]

In his full speech, printed in the appendix to the House journal, Moore said that

the prime movers in Abolition proceedings, and the great body of the intelligent signers to Abolition petitions, belong to the Federal school of politics.   They are consolidationists, and repudiate the doctrine of state rights.   They regard the powers of the federal government as omnipotent. . . .   The Federal or National Bank Party can believe nothing short of this. . . .

I would appeal to the journals of Congress—to the recorded votes of the members of this House on all test questions touching the subject of abolition.   I would appeal to the history of recent elections, and especially to the election in the state of New York, where it is well known every Abolitionist and Free Negro voted the Federal or Whig ticket.   Nay, more, I would appeal to the ten thousand abolition petitions with which this hall has been flooded for the last four years. . . .   [Among] the hundred thousand individuals that have signed petitions, praying for the abolition of slavery in the District of Columbia, there are not one hundred who are known to be friendly to the present Administration.   Who will, who can, who *dare* deny the truth of this assertion?

The long-term objective of an increasingly united Whig-Abolitionist Party Moore thought would find fruition when "the Southern Negro shall be brought to compete with the Northern white man in the labor market," and, when that happened, "the moral and political character, the pride, power, and independence, of the latter are gone forever."

But the New York Democrat did not believe his party would allow this to happen.   In a rare instance of a public admission that the Democrats acted *as a party* on the slavery issue, he added:

But let me tell you, Sir, the Democracy of the North and East are not unmindful of passing events.   Since abolitionism assumed a political character they have watched the movements of the Federal Abolition Party with deep concernment. . . .   Whenever the Democracy observe the Federal Party prosecuting a political measure with zeal and vigor, they unvoluntarily, instinctively gather up their energies to repel approaching mischief.[102]

Meanwhile, in the Senate, the burden under which the divided Whigs labored came to be too much for their leader Henry Clay to bear.   In a long speech, he unmistakably favored an end to abolitionist activity because of its danger to the Union, a danger which Clay felt more than most and which always brought out his instincts as a compromiser.[103]

Clay's plea for congressional unity in opposition to the abolitionists' crusade upset Northern Democrats who had withstood to some extent what was obviously the dominant sentiment in their own party.   Senator Morris of Ohio, while presenting some anti-slavery resolutions from his state, said

I informed my private friends of the political party with which I have hitherto acted, during the first week of this session, that these powers were forming a union to overthrow the present Administration; and I warned them of the folly and mischief they were doing in their abuse of those who were opposed to slavery.   All doubts are now terminated.   The display made by [Clay], and his denunciations of these petitioners as Abolitionists, and the hearty response and cordial embrace which his efforts met from [Calhoun] clearly shows that new moves have taken place on the political chessboard, and new coalitions are formed, new compromises and new bargains, settling and disposing of the rights of the country for the advantages of political aspirants.

---

[100] (December 11, 12, 1838) *ibid.* **7**: pp. 25, 27–28.   Four Southern Whigs voted against the gag, probably because the resolution was not extreme enough to satisfy them.
[101] (February 4, 1839) *ibid.* **7** (appendix): p. 241.

[102] *Ibid.*
[103] (February 7, 1839) **7** (appendix): pp. 354–359.

. . . What a lesson to the friends of the Administration, who have been throwing themselves into the arms of the Southern slave power for support! The black enchantment I hope is now at an end.[104]

[The slave power] is fast uniting together those opposed to its iron rule, no matter to what political party they have hitherto belonged.[105]

Morris's references to "the folly and mischief [the Democrats] were doing in their abuse of those opposed to slavery" and to "the friends of the Administration who have been throwing themselves into the arms of the Southern slave power for support" constitute the only recorded instance in all the congressional debates of the decade of a Northern Democrat rebuking his party for its overall position on slavery. Such a statement took courage to make. But Morris was also naive and myopic, though he may only have appeared to be in order to make certain points for their immediate political effect. In either case, his concern over the *possibility*—and at the time he spoke that is all it was—of a Whig—state rightist alliance in the South was hardly less worrisome than the prospect of such Northern Democrats as himself disassociating themselves from their party and joining with Northern Whigs. In either case, the abolitionists and the Southern extremists would have succeeded in pulling apart the national parties. The fearful prospect of the slavery issue sectionalizing a rather delicately balanced political system would then be a reality. The whole tone of Morris's speech is that he rather expected this to happen and may even have somehow wished it to happen.

1839–1840

Since 1840 was a presidential election year, the petitions controversy—along with everything else—took on a more noticeable political cast during the 1839–1840 session of Congress. Politicians were much more forthright in referring to the relationship between the slavery issue and the major parties. Speaker Polk and Vice-President Richard Johnson did not bother to rule long asides out of order.

The Whig strategy was simple and consistently maintained, at least for this session: Since the party was deeply divided, it was important to stress the nonpartisan character of the slavery problem, and, if this was not enough, to stress the abolitionists' influence on Northern Democrats in an effort to show the other party was not united either.[106] Representative Stanly from North Carolina "read the written opinions of some of the friends of the Administration [in the House] expressed at home and published in the newspapers of the day, for the purpose of identifying them with the cause of abolition. . . ."[107] Representative Botts of Virginia said that for all the talk about the "infection" of the House with abolitionist principles "there were [but] twenty in both parties [who were abolitionists' supporters and] thought that there were as many on one side as the other. If there were more he desired to know it, both for himself and his constituents. . . ."[108] Senator Tallmadge of New York insisted that Northern Whigs (or "conservative" renegades such as himself) and the abolitionists were distinct and separate, and those who claimed they were not were being politically irresponsible.[109]

When Whigs accused Northern Democrats of being abolitionists, the Democrats also reacted sharply. Bynum singled out Democratic Representative Parmenter of Massachusetts, who, in an extended exchange on the floor of the House, tried to explain that abolitionists wanted the slaves freed in the District and territories without regard for the consequences, whereas Massachusetts Democrats thought slavery was evil, to be sure, but would favor its abolition only if it could be done "without disturbing the peace and harmony of the Union, or violating the rights of others." In short, the abolitionists and the Democrats were distinct political groups, and one did not support the other for office.[110] When Whig Representative Peck of New York called Northern Democrats "Southern slaves," Democratic Representative Bynum of North Carolina said that Northern Whigs were abolitionists, something which started a shouting match. When Peck denied he was an abolitionist, Bynum called him a "blackguard" and a "scoundrel," but was later persuaded to apologize to the House for his language.[111]

Both Bynum and Democratic Representative Watterson from Tennessee gave long, detailed speeches on the evidence supporting the thesis of a growing collaboration between the Whigs and the abolitionists. And in the Senate, Brown of North Carolina did essentially the same thing, though on a smaller scale. All examined political activity, state by state, and presented voting statistics from earlier sessions of Congress on resolutions relating to slavery. And though the voting statistics and the state surveys were obviously selective, none of the three Democrats had any difficulty establishing a connection. They also pointed to Whig-dominated legislatures which regularly passed anti-slavery resolutions and to instances in which abolitionists publicly supported Whigs for office. The Whigs had also chosen as their presidential nominee a man who, in the view of their opponents, at least, had a highly ambiguous attitude

---

104 (February 9, 1839) *ibid.* **7** (appendix): p. 168.

105 (February 9, 1839) *ibid.* **7** (appendix): p. 171.

106 (Stanly of North Carolina, January 16, 1840; Botts of Virginia, January 16, 1840; Hunt of New York, January 23, 1840; Peck of New York, January 24, 1840; Johnson of Maryland, January 28, 1840, and Senator Tallmadge, "Conservative" from New York, February 13, 1840) *ibid.* **8**: pp. 125–126, 141, 142, 145, 150, 188.

107 (January 16, 1840) *ibid.* **8**: p. 125.

108 (January 16, 1840) *ibid.* **8**: p. 126.

109 (February 13, 1840) *ibid.* **8**: pp. 188, 189.

110 (January 16, 1840) *ibid.* **8**: p. 126.

111 (January 24, 1840) *ibid.* **8**: p. 145.

toward slavery. Harrison's earlier advocacy of the distribution of the surplus from the sale of public lands for abolition and colonization was frequently cited as solid evidence of his essentially anti-slavery posture.[112]

Senator Brown "believed there was not an intelligent Federalist in the Union, whatever opinions they may advance to the contrary, for political effect, that *did not know* the Abolitionists, as a body, were generally political auxiliaries of their own party, and enemies of the Democratic Party."[113] He added: "[Northern Whigs] know they cannot exist a day without panic, either in regard to banks, abolition, or something else; and now that all these other subjects have been worn out, they strive to get one upon the abstract right of petition, in order to enlist partisans under their banner."[114]

Democratic Senator Smith of Connecticut added a thoughtful analysis of why the Whigs had become mixed up with the anti-slavery movement. Smith believed the two-party system was natural and good for the American political system, but that only one of the major parties—the Democrats—had retained its principles and thus its cohesiveness over the years. The opposition parties, without either principles or cohesiveness, sought expedients and naturally attracted "sub-groups," such as the abolitionists. Though overstated, this essentially accurate insight Smith used to explain both the basic unity of the Democrats on such a divisive issue as slavery and the even more evident cooperation between Whigs and abolitionists. He added, rather inconsistently but also accurately, that "sub-groups" like the abolitionists blended into whichever party had principles closest to their own, an observation which suddenly gave to the Whigs a quality he had denied they possessed a few minutes before. In short, the abolitionists chose the Whigs because of the latter's attitude toward the use of governmental power.[115]

Bynum was particularly concerned about the inconsistent and partisan uses the Whigs made of the slavery issue. Northern Whigs ranted against a presumed Democratic denial of the right to petition. But Southern Whigs denounced Northern Democrats for supporting moderate, Southern-oriented resolutions, ignored their own Northern Whig colleagues who opposed *all* Southern interests, and spent their energy trying to identify individual Northern Democrats with the abolitionists.[116]

Bynum and Watterson both sharply contrasted Whig division with Democratic unity. They pointed with pride to Van Buren, whose position had been consistent throughout his presidency.

I rejoice [Watterson told his colleagues] that whilst this dark cloud of abolitionism is hanging over the country, that we have a pilot at the helm of state, whose views are so sound upon the subject that he has been denounced upon this floor as a "Northern man with Southern principles." If so, I yield to the justness of the denunciation.[117]

Bynum was more open than Watterson about the extent of Democratic *disunity*, however: "I daresay there are hundreds, perhaps thousands of Abolitionists in the Democratic Party. No man has ever denied there are some." But, he argued, until a majority are "infected," a party cannot be so *characterized*:

I am fully satisfied in my own mind that in the Democratic Party—and none are more sorry that it is so—there are from five to ten members here tinctured with abolitionism, and from the same kind, through much stronger evidence, it is my conscientious and solemn conviction, that there are from 65 to 75 Abolitionists in the Whig Party that hold seats on this floor; and I think I have shown, if deeds give character to men or parties, that a majority of that whole party in this House, from both North and South, if not open abolitionists, covertly act with them upon every occasion.[118]

Watterson went on to stress the positive side:

I assert that no man can be a Republican and an Abolitionist. The two terms are totally inconsistent, as much so as those of Democratic and Federalist. Gentlemen may specify a scattering Abolitionist, here and there, who occasionally cooperates with the Democratic Party, from local causes. But all his principles, feelings, and sympathies incline him toward the opposition. Moreover, the Democrats, as a party, have repudiated the doctrines of the Abolitionists. [The reference here is to the Calhoun and Atherton resolutions.] Look at the inaugural of the President, who stands pledged to veto any bill interfering with slavery in this District. Look at the address of the Democratic members of Congress to the people of the United States.[119] Look at their votes in the various state legislatures. Look at their resolves in their conventions, and in their primary meetings, and you will find abundant evidence of the truth of this assertion. Well did Mr. Jefferson remark, that the Democracy of the North are the natural allies of the South. Sir, I am proud of that alliance. We fight in one common cause and under one common banner. That cause is the constitution of our country. That banner is the same, which has so proudly waved over the Republican Party, from the foundation of this government.[120]

It is clear, therefore, that Bynum, Watterson, and Brown all sought to convince Southerners in an election year that the Democratic party, as a whole, was

---

[112] (Watterson, January 16, 1840; Bynum, January 25, 1840; and Brown, February 13, 1840) *ibid.* 8: pp. 146–147, 188; 8 (appendix): pp. 103–106, 257–264.

[113] (February 13, 1840) *ibid.* 8: p. 190.

[114] (February 13, 1840) *ibid.* 8: p. 189.

[115] (February 13, 1840) *ibid.* 8: p. 190.

[116] (January 25, 1840) *ibid.* 8 (appendix): p. 253. Representative Habersham, and state-rights Democrat from Georgia, made some of the same observations a day earlier. *Ibid.* 8: p. 145.

[117] (January 16, 1840) *ibid.* 8 (appendix): p. 104. Bynum expressed a similar view. (January 25, 1840) *ibid.* 8 (appendix): pp. 252–253.

[118] (January 25, 1840) *ibid.* 8 (appendix): p. 237.

[119] The Address was issued on July 6, 1838, at the end of the session during which the Senate passed Calhoun's resolutions, but before Atherton introduced his version in the House. The Address was repeated by Watterson at the end of his long speech. (January 16, 1840) *ibid.* 8 (appendix): p. 106.

[120] (January 16, 1840) *ibid.* 8 (appendix): p. 104.

far more oriented toward Southern interests than the Whigs.[121]

Two state rightists from Georgia who were elected to the House as Whigs, but who became independents during the 1839–1840 session, also commented on the parties and slavery, but from the outsider's point of view. "I am neither Whig nor Democrat, and can be excused, therefore, from compromising our rights to secure votes for their friends. I will speak with boldness my thoughts, and deal out blows against the foes of Constitutional right, no matter to which party they may belong." So proclaimed Representative Colquitt, who went on to explain with rare candor just what drove a Southern Whig out of the party:

We are told not to be rash; make ourselves easy; treat them with respect; and by it our friends from the North will again be elected, and "all's well." The very entreaties that are uttered, and the strong appeals of party associates, which are made, are convincing proofs that they are courting the friendship of the abolitionists for their votes.[122]

Both Colquitt and his Georgia colleague, Cooper, were "satisfied there are Abolitionists of both parties; and that party which courts them most, is by the American people most to be blamed."[123] Cooper added that "one party, as a whole, is by profession and practice somewhat more friendly to our interest, on this question, than the other, resulting mainly from their respective positions; but either seem hitherto to have fixed limits short of what our rights and the Constitution authorize them to go."[124] Colquitt's solution was for all Whigs and Democrats to "tear loose from the bonds of any party, no matter what their ties," and oppose all proposals which would upset the peace and harmony of the Union.[125]

But other state rightists rejected the non-party approach. The small group of Southern Democrats who associated with Calhoun, when asked, publicly stated why they decided to support the administration party. Representative Butler of South Carolina said "we are not . . . partisans of the Administration nor do we intend to become so. We support the leading measures of the Administration because we believe them to be calculated to promote the best interests of the country."[126] Butler went on to catalog the ways in which the Democrats were friendly toward Southern interests.[127]

It was Calhoun himself who best expressed the essential relationship between abolition and the major parties at the end of the decade:

I understand this whole question. The great mass of both parties to the North are opposed to abolition: the Democrats almost exclusively; the Whigs, less so. Very few are to be found in the ranks of the former; but many in that of the latter. The only importance that the Abolitionists have, is to be found in the fact that their weight may be felt in elections; and this is no small advantage. The one party is unwilling to lose their weight, but, at the same time, unwilling to be blended with them on the main question; and hence is made this false, absurd, unconstitutional, and dangerous collateral issue on the right of petition. Here is the whole secret. They are willing to play the political game at our hazard and that of the Constitution and the Union, for the sake of victory at the elections.[128]

Calhoun here again exhibited the insight which his small band of extremists first articulated in the mid-thirties. By operating within the party which was most strongly anti-abolitionist he obviated the criticism made earlier against the creation of a separate "Southern" party which could not combat abolitionist tendencies in the North itself.

Even the number of Northern Democrats opposed to the gag rule declined in this most "political" of years, by about one-third to ten. Seven were from New England, two from New York, and one from the Mid-West. Since both of the New Yorkers resigned and the Indianian was defeated in the next election, Democratic defections were virtually a New England phenomenon.[129]

CONCLUSION

What complicates the relationship between party loyalty and the slavery issue in the 1830's is the imprecise definition "abolition" or "abolitionist" were given by politicians who used the terms typically for partisan purposes. There was no one in Congress who publicly favored abolition everywhere. And even those who were sympathetic in that they were in some sense "anti-slavery" cannot be clearly identified or counted year by year, the reason being that for some who voted against the gag rule the right of petition was what they were concerned about, while their attitude toward slavery was left ambiguous. Ambiguous too was the meaning of the many resolutions pertaining to the petitions presented to the House or the Senate during these years. Much of the debate turned on a lack of agreement on what the actual relationship between Congress and its handling of petitions would be if this or that resolution were accepted. There was even confusion at times over what a particular congressman's vote signified, as some voted "no" because a particular resolution was not extreme enough. For instance this is what happened

---

[121] (Bynum, January 24, 25, 1840; Brown, February 13, 1840) *ibid.* **8**: pp. 145, 188; **8** (appendix): p. 257.
[122] (January 17, 1840) *ibid.* **8** (appendix): p. 144.
[123] *Ibid.*
[124] (January 16, 1840) *ibid.* **8** (appendix): p. 102.
[125] (January 17, 1840) *ibid.* **8** (appendix): p. 144.
[126] (January 21, 1840) *ibid.* **8**: p. 132.
[127] (January 21, 1840) *ibid.* **8** (appendix): p. 109.

[128] (February 13, 1840) *ibid.* **8**: p. 188.
[129] (January 13, 1840) *ibid.* **8**: pp. 119–120.

when Whig Representative Crabb voted against one of the annual gag resolutions. According to Crabb, an abolitionists' newspaper announced he was simply opposed to the gag, a charge transferred to "an Administration newspaper in his district, and used in elections against him."[130]

But even with this lack of clarity and precision certain facts emerge. The Whigs were deeply divided over slavery along sectional lines from their birth as a party. By contrast, the Democrats, with a longer history and with a leadership determined to keep the slavery issue out of politics, were generally united in opposition to the anti-slavery movement. Those Northern Democrats who opposed the imposition of a gag rule declined somewhat during the decade, but there is no evidence of an attempted "purge" or, indeed, of a direct linkage between the presentation of anti-slavery petitions and an anti-party voting record. In the meantime, the state-rights extremists were satisfied with the reception that first Calhoun's and then Atherton's resolutions got and thereafter voted with their erstwhile colleagues.

There was also a rather close connection between state and national political activity on the slavery issue in the thirties. When state legislatures passed resolutions of either an anti- or pro-slavery character, the party divisions were of the same character as in Congress, even including small groups of renegade Democrats.[131] But it would be a mistake to conclude that state action determined in any significant way congressional voting patterns. The initial divisions in Congress occurred before state legislatures passed resolutions with any regularity. And the fact that relatively few of the renegade Democrats either resigned or were defeated in the next election is fairly sound evidence that the reason they adopted their anti-party posture was because of pressure from their constituents. In other words, it would have been politically disastrous to have taken the same position as the rest of their party colleagues.

What did change in these years, especially by the time of the presidential election of 1840, was the willingness of congressmen to talk about the relationship between party politics and the slavery issue, something which was true of other issues as well, however.

PUBLIC LANDS

Henry Clay's scheme for the distribution of the proceeds of the public land to the states according to the size of their congressional delegation provoked continuing congressional debate from 1832 to 1836. The "distribution" issue produced, unlike the tariff and internal improvements, an obvious party division, but

of an uneven kind. From the beginning, the "opposition" was virtually unanimous in its support for Clay's proposal. But, the administration party was divided, with a sizable majority against the measure, however. Why the difference? One factor was that Clay, the most influential of those who opposed Jackson, made distribution a matter of great personal concern. In June, 1832, when the subject was first debated, he told his colleagues (with characteristic exaggeration) that:

No subject which had presented itself to the present, or perhaps any preceding Congress, was of greater magnitude than that of public lands. . . . Long after we shall cease to be agitated by the tariff, ages after our manufactures shall have acquired a stability and perfection which will enable them successfully to cope with the manufactures of any other country, the public lands will remain a subject of deep and enduring interest. As to their extent there is public land enough to found an empire. . . . We may safely . . . anticipate that long, if not centuries after the present day, the representatives of our children may be deliberating in the halls of Congress on laws relating to the public lands.[132]

The importance he attached to his scheme can be gauged from a comment to a friend after the continued failure of Congress to pass a distribution bill:

I have not decided [he wrote in May, 1833] whether I shall return to the Senate or not. If the land bill had passed I certainly should not have gone there again; and the condition in which that measure has been left, creates the only doubt which I feel. . . . Twice have I pressed the bill in the Senate, where it has twice passed, and once in the House. . . . [The] public lands will be lost to the country, without some such measure is adopted. They will be used as an instrument to advance the ambitious views of some Presidential aspirant, by offering motives to the new states to support him.[133]

One does not have to regard Clay as one wholly uninvolved in the "political" aspects of the government's public-lands policies to discern his obvious personal association with a particular proposal relating to those policies.

Clay's personal leadership was one factor making for opposition party unity. In addition, the very nature of his proposal was such that it was relatively easy for those in opposition to Jackson to rally round. Though no one said so in debate on the subject, the bill provided a general scheme which did not leave any room for "log-rolling"—positions taken under pressure from constituents, with local needs and interests in view—something which marked discussions on innumerable tariff and internal improvements bills. The question to be decided was simply whether or not the people's representatives wanted the federal government or the state governments to spend the money collected from the sale of the public lands. Thus, it is not surprising that debate on Clay's bill was generally without references to local considerations. In short, those who

[130] (January 15, 1840) *ibid.* **8**: p. 123.
[131] For example, New York State. (Senator Wright's remarks, February 13, 1840) *ibid.* **8**: p. 192.
[132] (June 20, 1832) *Register of Debates* **8**: p. 1098.
[133] (May 30, 1833) Clay to Francis Brooke, *Clay Correspondence*, pp. 361–362.

opposed Jackson could support Clay on a proposal in which general, national, or more precisely, party interests were paramount.

Jackson's initial advocacy of a distribution bill has already been referred to. As if in response to the President's failure to mention the subject in his third Annual Message, Clay introduced a distribution bill during the session that followed. Though some, such as Senator Grundy of Tennessee "thought the subject should be considered at home, before it was submitted to Congress, [as] it was now for the first time brought here,"[134] the Senate, at least, passed the measure by a vote of 26–18. The identifiable Jacksonians split; nine supported it, while sixteen were in opposition. By contrast clear opponents of the administration (twelve in number) were unanimously in favor.[135]

In his fourth Annual Message, in December, 1832, the President, perhaps mindful that a sizable majority of those who supported him in the Senate had voted against distribution, shifted his attention to the prospect of removing the sale of public lands as a source of revenue, once the public debt was extinguished within the next year or two.[136] In other words, Jackson suggested that Congress examine the possibility of free lands for settlers. Undaunted, Clay reintroduced the distribution bill, and the Senate quickly passed it, with the same nine Jacksonians voting affirmatively.[137] The bill's managers in the House were able to force a vote at the very end of the session, with many representatives absent. The lopsided result, 96–39 in favor, suggests that those who felt strongly about the proposal remained for a showdown. But even in this reduced legislature, administration supporters divided 37–33 in support of a measure the President had recommended several years before. Only three identifiable opposition members opposed what Clay so strongly favored.[138]

Jackson, at this point, must have been in a dilemma. Clay, who had emerged as his leading political opponent during the debate over the bank recharter bill and who was to be nominated by the "National Republicans" had usurped a proposal originally made by the President. The question was: Now that Congress had passed a distribution bill, should Jackson sign it or not? If he did, he would be acting in accordance with his own suggestions, but would alienate a significant segment of those who had been admini-

stration supporters. If he did not, he would risk the charge of doing what was politically expedient and presumably inconsistent. At the same time, he would alienate other supporters. Jackson's solution was astute and characteristic: He vetoed the bill because of specific provisions within it which he found unconstitutional, at the same time that he held out hope for a similar act shorn of the improper provisions.[139] Specifically, the President referred to the sections in the bill which required the state governments to spend a portion of the funds allotted to them on internal improvements and education and which allowed them to spend the remainder on anything they deemed proper. Jackson found these provisions repugnant to the constitutional position he articulated in his veto of the Maysville Road bill: "If the money of the United States can not be applied to local projects *through its own agents*, as little can it be permitted to be thus expended *through the agency of the state governments.*"[140]

The vote on Clay's bill revealed the extent to which, for the opposition at least, distribution had become a party issue. The Jacksonians, of course, realized this, and regretted it, largely because they were not united. The *Globe*, their party journal in Washington, noted at the outset of the next session that "the disposition of the public lands will occupy much of the public attention during the present winter; the more so, because the subject is evidently becoming political and falling into the vortex of party politics. . . . The subject was sufficiently difficult and delicate without the super-addition of political considerations."[141] This, at virtually the same time that Clay was telling a friend he would stay in the Senate if only to lead the fight for a distribution law. But, instead, the protracted debate on the deposits system for government revenues dominated the session. It was not until the 1835–1836 session that another distribution measure was considered by both sessions of Congress. By that time, parties had become fairly well established and a presidential election was imminent.

But even in this more pronounced partisan atmosphere, Democrats, mindful of earlier divisions, asked that the issue be viewed on its merits. Senator Ewing of Ohio, who was to vote against the measure, said that "[there] was no reason why this bill should be made a party question. On former occasions, several Senators who were party men and friends of the Administration had voted for it."[142] Senator Isaac Hill, long a party stalwart, prefaced his remarks with the statement that

I have consulted on this subject with none. An ardent friend of this Administration, I would do nothing to injure it or its friends; for the opinions I have now offered, the

[134] (July 2, 1832) *Register of Debates* 8: p. 1161.
[135] *Ibid.* 8: p. 1174.
[136] Richardson, editor, *Messages and Papers* 3: pp. 1163–1166.
[137] *Register of Debates* 9: p. 235. The vote was 24–20.
[138] *Ibid.* 9: pp. 1920–1921. A breakdown of the vote reveals precisely the nature of the Democratic division:

	N.Y.	Pa.	Ohio	Va.	Ky.	Tenn.	N.C.	S.C.
For	8	12	6	3	2	0	2	0
Against	3	1	0	9	3	2	3	2
	Al.	Ind.	Ill.	Me.	Mo.	La.	R.I.	Ga.
For	0	0	0	1	1	1	1	0
Against	3	2	1	0	1	0	0	1

[139] Richardson, editor, *Messages and Papers* 3: pp. 1282–1288.
[140] *Ibid.*, p. 1285.
[141] *Washington Globe*, December 11, 1833.
[142] (March 15, 1836) *Congressional Globe* 3: pp. 233–234.

Administration is not responsible. If my suggestions are worthy of attention, they will doubtless have their due weight; if they are unworthy, they can injure no one but myself.[143]

Even the *National Intelligencer*, the Whig party journal in Washington, when it reviewed the favorable vote in the Senate, where all Whigs voted affirmatively, could afford to take a charitable view of the proceedings:

What was remarkable . . . was that [the debate] was wholly divested of a party character, and involved in argument only such considerations as were suggested by a regard to public expediency and the security of the public money. If any other element entered into the motive of the great majority of the Senate on this occasion, it was at least not visible on the surface; and we are bound to presume that none other existed.[144]

But the *Globe* did not share this interpretation. Ever sensitive to the activity of the opposition, its editor, Francis Blair, laced his editorials during the weeks the new distribution bill was being debated with admonitions to administration supporters that Clay's party had made both the land distribution and bank deposits questions party issues:

The bank party, forever appealing to mercenary motives, now in effect proposes through its advocates in Congress to purchase the states by the dividends of the Treasury. . . . The men in Congress who have already clogged the general government in its action . . . are thus anxiously pressing on the cupidity of state politicians the vast bribes of the land bill and surplus dividends, to induce the adoption of their party schemes. This is the price the states must pay for the great bonus held out by the bank politicians. . . . The states will be thus rendered dependent on the general government, and the general government will be thrown in the hands of a corrupt party . . . with [it] the only source of political power. This was Hamilton's doctrine. . . . This is the system of his followers of the present day: Clay, Biddle, Webster, and all their associates.[145]

Blair went on to accuse the Whigs of: (1) purposefully delaying action on appropriation bills to create the impression that there was a great surplus; (2) deliberately stalling action on legislative proposals so that the Whigs could argue the Democratic-controlled Congress had not attended to the people's business; (3) trying to create another panic by keeping public money out of circulation; (4) seeking to establish a five-year distribution scheme which would lead to an increase in tariff duties; and (5) attempting to increase the power of state politicians (who would spend the surplus) at the expense of the public's welfare.[146] Senator Benton detected an attempt on the part of Jackson's opponents to destroy the President's popularity, by forcing him to veto a bill which was popular. But Benton also thought the voters

would recognize the purely political motivaton of the Whigs.[147]

The Whigs, in turn, feared the unrestrained power of the executive if it continued to control the fast-growing government deposits in state banks chosen because of their political loyalty. As Representative Chilton Allen of Kentucky put it:

The weighty contest now depending before Congress and before the nation is, whether the [surplus], which is the produce of the honest labor of our constituents, shall be returned to their pockets, or devoted to the schemes of official ambition upon the eve of a Presidential election. In this aspect of the question, it bears directly upon all the great interests of the nation, and upon the interest and liberty of every man in the nation.[148]

The *National Intelligencer* made the same point in an editorial on April 28:

The surplus money in the deposit banks continues to increase, . . . subject to the absolute and uncontrolled pleasure of the President of the United States as to the particular banks who shall enjoy the advantages of these deposits, the amount of which in some instances far exceeds the whole capital of the bank. Is it possible that Congress can think of adjourning and leaving things in this state?

Allen went on to accuse Jackson of fostering the growth of parties in Congress, even though it is unlikely Allen was unaware that the Democrats had not previously been united on the distribution issue, which suggests that he feared such a development. "Has this Administration wielded its power to crush the monster called party spirit?" he asked.

On the contrary, has not this fell monster been nourished and fed until it has become a bloated juggernaut, whose voracious appetite has not been satisfied with a thousand victims of the opposite party, but has, without pity or remorse, crushed beneath its ponderous wheels almost all its original votaries? Must not all worship at the shrine of this idol, under pain of their proscription and unrelenting prosecution?[149]

On May 14, the Senate passed a distribution bill by a vote of 25–20, with all opposition senators voting affirmatively.[150] Five Democrats joined them. Pennsylvania's two senators were under instructions to do so,[151] which meant that three administration supporters out of twenty-four who voted, did not support party unity: Senators Black (Mississippi), Nicholas (Louisiana), and Preston (South Carolina).

The *Intelligencer* expressed its pleasure over the Senate's action and hoped Jackson would sign the bill if it also passed the House. Considering the "vast" surplus and the popular sentiment favoring such a measure, the journal's editors thought conditions had changed sufficiently since the President's veto in 1833

---

[143] (March 17, 1836) *ibid*. **3** (appendix): p. 181.
[144] *National Intelligencer*, June 20, 1836.
[145] *Washington Globe*, April 29, 1836.
[146] *Ibid*., March 2, April 23, May 2, 4, 26, June 14, 15, 21, 1836.

[147] (April 27, 1836) *Congressional Globe* **3** (appendix): p. 315.
[148] (March 21, 1836) *ibid*. **3** (appendix): p. 598.
[149] (March 21, 1836) *ibid*. **3** (appendix): p. 598.
[150] *Ibid*. **3**: p. 342.
[151] *Ibid*. **3** (appendix): p. 610.

for him to change his position.[152]   But Representative Bynum, a loyal Democrat from North Carolina, thought Jackson would veto the bill even if it received the House's approval.   After all, the measure the House received was quite similar to the one the President had vetoed.[153]

On June 16, however, the House refused to table the bill by a vote of 110–96.   Thirty Democrats out of the 117 voting sided with the Whigs.   Most of the dissidents were from five states: Pennsylvania (9), North Carolina (5), Virginia (3), and Indiana (3).[154] A day later the Senate passed overwhelmingly—40–6—a modified version of its own distribution bill.   The *Intelligencer* thought the "majority so great as to leave no doubt that it will also pass the House of Representatives."[155]

What, then, would Jackson do?   Would he veto a bill which had won such broad support in the Senate and might well be popular in the House as well.   The President must have mulled over the matter for a few days.   On June 21, he acted.   The House, dramatically reversing itself, voted to table the distribution bill, and there is no doubt it did so because the President had suggested a compromise amendment.   In a revealing letter to Jackson written in the Capitol at 6 P.M. on June 21, Democratic Senator Richard M. Johnson told the President:

I have never witnessed such rejoicing, as I have this day among our friends; as soon as I gave assurances to most of them, that you would approve of the deposit principle, with the states; but that you would veto a bonus, or loaning, as specified.   The amendment embracing your suggestions went like wildfire. . . .   We have carried the amendment by a majority of all the 240 members [,] say 127–50.[156]

Clearly Jackson, sensing defeat if he persisted and vetoed another distribution scheme, sought to retain his political leadership by taking the initiative away from Clay and let it be known he supported another scheme which he evidently hoped would be palatable to both Democrats and Whigs.   At any rate, eleven of the thirty Democrats who had opposed tabling Clay's distribution bill voted to do so on June 22, and the motion passed, 104–85.   Though there is no direct evidence, it seems likely that the President's maneuver was influential in reducing the number of renegade Democrats from thirty to sixteen, permitting the tabling of the original bill.

The *Globe*, quickly reversing its opposition to distribution, explained the President's proposal: The state governments were to be depositories of public money over $5,000,000 in amount.   But they were to be depositories only; the money was not to be a gift or a loan.   Jackson would have vetoed Clay's Senate bill because distribution was uneconomical as a means of taxation and unpolitic in that it would create a bureaucracy.[157]

But the *Intelligencer* was not satisfied with this explanation of Jackson's conduct.   Recapitulating what had happened, the journal's editors indicated that when Clay's bill passed the Senate, Democrats in the House asserted Jackson would again veto the measure if the House disapproved, "but the favor it received in the House, from the moment of its introduction, added to the powerful vote by which it passed the Senate, threw consternation and confusion into the ranks of those who would willingly have contributed to defeat it [either in the House or in the "palace"].   It became necessary to find or make some cause of action, upon which the President might change his course, and sign a bill, which [if] it had inconsiderately [been] given out he would arrest by the exercise of the veto power."   The President then had friends announce his support of Anthony's amendment.   It is generally believed that the amendment "was actually drawn up, after much consultation, by a member of the cabinet."   The bill now passed "makes the states pledge their faith for repayment, without providing any means for enforcing a demand" that they do so.   "No one seriously expects the states to restore the deposits to the federal government."[158]

The *Intelligencer's* account appears to be a far more accurate version of what happened than the *Globe's*, whose editors had the embarrassing task of supporting a bill which they had vociferously opposed, something their rival editors took great delight in pointing out.[159] One does not have to accept the assertion that a member of the Cabinet actually wrote Anthony's amendment in order to accept the *Intelligencer's* claim that Jackson approved a compromise measure which would allow him to retain some control over the direction of legislation in Congress.   His prestige would not have withstood an overridden veto.

The President's party exhibited the same lack of unity on the "preemption" and "graduation" issues that was evident with respect to distribution measures.   On early bills "to prohibit the sale of public land except to actual settlers" (preemption), Democratic division was as prominent as on other issues involving the public lands.   In 1837 six administration supporters in the Senate joined with the opposition in an unsuccessful attempt to adjourn without taking action

[152] *National Intelligencer*, May 5, 1836.
[153] (May 12, 1836) *Congressional Globe* 3: p. 369.
[154] *Ibid.* 3: p. 450.   Pennsylvania's representatives were requested by the state legislature to vote for the bill.   *Ibid.* 3 (appendix): p.610.
[155] *National Intelligencer*, June 18, 1836.
[156] (June 21, 1836) R. M. Johnson to Jackson, *Jackson Correspondence* 5: p. 409.   Democratic Representative Anthony of Pennsylvania introduced an amendment embodying the President's suggestions, and it passed easily, 155–38.   *Congressional Globe* 3: p. 459.
[157] *Washington Globe*, June 24, 1836.
[158] *National Intelligencer*, June 25, 1836.
[159] *Ibid.*, June 27, 1836.

on a preemption measure.[160] A year later five voted with the Whigs against passage of a similar measure.[161] In the House, thirty-three out of the 107 who supported a motion to table a preemption bill measure in March, 1873, were Democrats, while eight were in opposition. Twelve out of Virginia's eighteen Democrats were among the thirty-three, along with four out of six North Carolina Democrats, all four of South Carolina's "states rights" Democrats, and four out of Ohio's nine Democrats. Only eleven Whigs—scattered through seven delegations—broke ranks and voted against the bill.[162]

And yet, just a year later some rather dramatic shifts in the voting patterns occurred. The Whigs suddenly lost their virtual unanimity when thirty-five joined with ninety-seven Democrats to enact another preemption bill. Eight out of Tennessee's ten Whigs were among the thirty-five, half of Kentucky's and Pennsylvania's ten Whigs, and all but one of Indiana's six Whigs. Only sixteen Democrats voted against the bill, whereas thirty-three had opposed the earlier measure. The center of opposition remained in the South Atlantic states, though the Virginians involved shrank to six and only one of the renegades was from a Northern state.[163]

What accounts for this? Two new developments undoubtedly influenced the voting. One was Van Buren's recommendation—the first by any president— that Congress enact a preemption law.[164] Five Virginians who had voted to delay action on the 1837 preemption bill voted in favor of the 1838 one (Craig, Dromgoole, Hopkins, Joseph Johnson, and Morgan) and one Northern representative did likewise (Buchanan of Pennsylvania). The President's endorsement may well have induced their change of position. The other factor—already in evidence during the 1837 discussion—was a growing East-West division. Chairman of the House Public Lands Committee Ratliff Boon, Democrat from Indiana, and William May, Democrat from Illinois, reportedly got into an "altercation" over whether or not preemption should in fact be a party question. Joseph Randolph, Whig from New Jersey, who referred to the clash, told his House colleagues: "I do not myself consider the present question a political question. It is one of those matters in which the whole country is interested, and which . . . should be paramount to mere party consideration. The controversy . . . as I understand it, is rather between the old and the new states."[165] One does not have to deny altogether the influence of party in order to perceive

the influence of geography on the voting: Practically all the Democrats who opposed the bill were from the East coast; nearly all the Whigs who favored it were Westerners.

Thus, both the distribution and preemption issues produced voting patterns that represented an amalgam of influences from party, section, and locality. As such, the whole debate over the public lands in the thirties was a kind of model for all the other controversies.

THE BANK

Arthur Schlesinger, Jr., was right: the bank issue was *the* political issue of the 1830's. But it was more than that. It was also *the* party issue. Both voting records and the substance of debates on charter renewal, deposit banks, and independent treasury bills reveal unmistakably that politicians in Washington regarded positions on banking to be fundamental to party affiliation and identity. It is not an exaggeration to state that, as in the 1790's, two major parties were formed in Congress as a result of divisions created by banking legislation. Those who supported President Jackson and those who opposed him found their identity as legislators, and not just as candidates at election time, when both Jackson and Clay insisted on and received the loyalty of their supporters. Nothing indicates the unique political character of the banking issue so well as the fate of those Democrats who opposed the Independent Treasury scheme of the late 1830's. They did not ask for allowance of diversity, as Democrats had on all other issues. They simply left the party.

Why was the banking issue of such fundamental importance, not once, but twice, in our history? As early as 1832, Georgia Representative James Wayne, who opposed the bank re-charter bill, told his colleagues that "the tariff was a matter of mere sectional interests, while the bank was a question more simple and more general."[166] Two years later, in the midst of the debate over the deposit banks, at the very moment that the opposition took on the name Whig, Senator Thomas Hart Benton uttered what must be the classic explanation for the preeminence of banking proposals as a party issue:

Mr. B remarked on the political character of this bank. He said it was born a political institution, and was the first measure of the government to develop the line which so long and so distinctly marked the political parties of this country. The creation of the bank went to the origin of party. It went to the source where parties should be formed—to principles, to great and fundamental principles in the Administration of government. It involved the question of constructive and of granted powers; and was the entering wedge to all the implied powers afterwards assumed by Congress. Prohibitory tariffs—local internal improvement—and the whole American system. He said the bank was the head of the American system;

---

[160] *Congressional Globe* 4: p. 145. Four others abstained. The vote was 20–26.

[161] *Ibid.* 6: p.149. Again, four abstained. The vote on passage was 30–18.

[162] *Ibid.* 5: p.216.

[163] *Ibid.* 6: p. 452.

[164] Richardson, editor, *Messages and Papers* 4: p. 1606.

[165] (June 12, 1838) *Congressional Globe* 6 (appendix): p. 500.

[166] (June 30, 1832) *Register of Debates* 8: p. 3836.

and if it was rechartered, it would reestablish that system in greater power and glory than it ever possessed. . . . He warned gentlemen who were opposed to the American system not now to reestablish this eldest and strongest member of that system; and which, if reestablished, would certainly set up the whole family again. . . . The political grammar . . . is now strangely confused. Many men have got into the wrong places. They wear the name of one party, and act on the principles of the other. Parties . . . were ring-streaked, and speckled. This was their state now; but this bank question, carrying all back to the year 1791—ascending to the true fountain of party distinction—would set all right, and come back to the two plain colors, which would be a true index to everyone's political principles. Bank or no bank will be the question for years to come.[167]

Four years later the *Globe* was still making essentially the same point:

It is curious that the controversy which agitated the community so strongly forty years ago, is now revived with more energy than ever. The bank was the first great question which alienated the Republicans from their opponents; and it still draws the strongest line between the two parties. That violation of the Constitution by which the first bank was sanctioned was the entering wedge for the dangerous doctrine of loose construction, whence has proceeded every subsequent encroachment upon the rights of the states. Protective tariff, internal improvements by the general government, all the spurious progeny of latitudinarian doctrines, derive their origin from this source.[168]

And two years later, during the debate over the Independent Treasury bill, Representative Edward Black, a Democrat from Georgia, added: "This, at least, is an issue for the *public eye:* an Independent Treasury, or a United States Bank. Either is the only alternative of the other, and between them the people are called upon to choose."[169]

Even before the session during which the Democrats and Whigs assumed their formal identity began, the editor of the Washington *Globe* was aware of the way in which the bank deposits issue would be used as the basis for nothing less than the creation of a new party:

The opposition in Congress do not expect . . . to effect a restoration of the deposits. The struggle is made only to *rally, enlist,* and confirm a party under the standard of the bank, Clay, and Calhoun, in each branch of Congress against the President. Those who vote with

them on the deposits, they expect, will be associated with them in public opinion, and driven into their ranks for future use. It is to give the coalition against the President and the Democracy *a show of strength*—which they trust to circumstances—to bank management—and political intrigue, to make real and permanent. Once committed against the Administration upon so vital a question as that which now agitates the country, and our adroit national and nullifier have little doubt of securing forever to their cause, all who may so far espouse it.[170]

Members of the opposition in turn accused the Jackson administration of attempting to make the Bank of the United States as subservient to the Democratic party as the administration had already made the Post Office Department, whose workers seemed to wear collars with the inscription, "Andrew Jackson, his dog." But the Bank, under Nicholas Biddle's leadership, had refused to become the tool of any party.[171] Democrats repeatedly identified the opposition as the "bank party," however,[172] and were much closer to the truth. Jackson did not seek to control the Bank; he sought to destroy it as a national institution. The emergent opposition defended it, and indeed created a sense of common identity in Congress out of loyalty to it.

But there is no doubt that Jackson made the bank deposits issue the first important test of party loyalty among those who had campaigned in 1832 in support of his candidacy. With rare candor, Representative John King of Georgia revealed to the House what had happened. King, elected as a Democrat, traveled through his district and state before the 1833–1834 session began, and found the people favored the administration, but did not support removal of the deposits from the Bank of the United States:

I thought these were the sentiments of a majority even of the friends of the Administration when Congress assembled, and if the question of restoration had been viewed only as one of expediency—had not been made a party question, and forced upon the friends of the Administration, which was preferred for higher reasons, was to depend, and a vote taken on the subject before these apprehended mischiefs had occurred . . . a majority of two-thirds of both Houses, might have voted a restoration of the deposits.[173]

Though undoubtedly an exaggerated assessment of the situation, King's statement indicates clearly that the President's insistence on party loyalty was a wrenching experience for legislators not at all accustomed to such demands. King even drew back from any close association between party and the actions taken by individual representatives: "By what authority," he asked, "do gentlemen so connect a party with me as to embarrass it either by my statements or admissions?"[174] All this contrasts rather starkly with the

[167] (April 3, 1834) *Congressional Globe* 1: pp. 285–286.
[168] *Washington Globe,* January 1, 1838. If those who argued in this manner had been entirely consistent, they would have favored making the tariff and internal improvements—which they also regarded as parts of the so-called "American System"—party issues as well. There is no doubt that a number of Democrats in the thirties thought Clay's "American System" was simply an up-dated, modified, or extended version of Hamilton's "program" of the 1790's. That neither Benton nor the *Globe* ever went on record in support of a unified Democratic position on either the tariff or internal improvements is convincing evidence that considerations other than party loyalty were paramount on these issues, even though both the Senator and Blair were aware of the overall relationship of the tariff and internal improvements to the bank issue.
[169] (June 15, 16, 1840) *Congressional Globe* 8 (appendix): p. 694.
[170] *Washington Globe,* December 30, 1833.
[171] Remarks of Representative Hardin of Kentucky. (April 1, 1834) *Congressional Globe* 1: p. 284.
[172] For example: Representative Black of Georgia. (June 15, 1840) *ibid.* 8: p. 467.
[173] (March 12, 1834) *Ibid.* 1: pp. 231–232.
[174] *Ibid.*

statement of a renegade Whig from the same state made six years later, during the debate on the Independent Treasury bill in the spring of 1840. Representative E. J. Black, a "state's rights" Whig, told his colleagues:

> Sir, I accept the designation; it is emphatically "the measure of the Administration"; and upon that measure mainly, I go to the support of Mr. Van Buren. Upon that measure he must stand or fall in the pending contest; for while there are many other grounds upon which I am compelled to support him in obedience to principle, the Independent Treasury system stands out prominently and preeminently as *the* measure on which he rests his claims to the suffrages of his countrymen. . . . "*A national bank*" is the great measure of the Whig Party. . . . This brief statement constitutes the great issue joined between the two contending parties, and which is shortly to be submitted to the final judgment of the people of this country.[175]

1832–1833

The first bank recharter bill, of 1832, did not unite Jackson supporters, though most who opposed him supported the bill. Congressional leaders knew long before the actual vote that the bill would pass. Clay wrote to a friend in the early stages of the debate on the measure: "The impression now is, that the bank charter will pass at this session."[176] And later: "The bank bill will, I think pass the Senate in a few days . . . ."[177] Jackson's supporters, sensing defeat, argued that though the bill ought to be discussed, a decision should be postponed until other, more pressing proposals, had been acted on, so that the public could have time to think about the merits and the demerits of recharter.[178] Representative John Thomson, a Jacksonian from Ohio, told his colleagues that

> when he was elected to this House, he had not expected to be called to vote on this question, nor had his constituents expected any such thing. He had been taken by surprise; his constituents had been taken by surprise. Mr. T said it was impossible that the House could with any propriety pass the bill at this session. For himself he was uninstructed.[179]

But those who supported the bill disagreed. Senator Alexander Buckner of Missouri wondered why the other matters before Congress should not be postponed and why this form of inaction should not be adopted whenever a controversial question appeared. Why make a special case of the Bank?[180] Senator Alexander Dallas of Pennsylvania, nominally a Jackson supporter, but instructed by his state's legislature to vote for recharter, urged congressional action before the end of the session. In his first Annual Message,

the President had invited the people to consider the future of the Bank of the United States. They had done so, as was demonstrated by the large number of petitions and memorials submitted to Congress by individuals and corporations and by the legislative resolutions favoring renewal from various parts of the country.[181] Dallas's remarks prompted Senator Charles Dudley, a Jacksonian from New York, to indicate he would willingly obey the instructions which he presented from his legislature, which were in opposition to renewal.[182]

Opponents of the bill were convinced that it had been introduced as a party measure. Benton insisted that Congress did not know the administration's views on the matter and that the adversaries of the administration were forcing legislation on it, without consulting it:

> This very bank may be an enemy to the present Administration, and, uniting with all the elements of opposition in Congress, may now be exerting its tremendous influence . . . in favor of a new Administration which would keep up taxes, multiply expenditures, and gorge it with public money. . . . Some have said this push for a new charter is not a party measure, but thus far it had been characterized by every circumstance that defines a party measure; and this determination to carry it through, without reference to the Administration, seems to complete the evidence of that character.[183]

Another Jacksonian, Senator Isaac Hill of New Hampshire, said that agents of the Bank of the United States in his state had used power and influence in support of John Quincy Adams, as long ago as 1828, even before Jackson had indicated his position on banks:

> The party opposed to the Administration has compelled the bank to take its ground at this time. The "newspapers" and the "demagogues" of the party make this bank the ground of the opposition. . . . The friends of the President, while they regret that this is really a party question exclusively, on one side, and a divided question in some sections of the country, on the other, have no fears for the results. . . .[184]

The bill's supporters, confident of victory and certain that the President's supporters would not unite, simply denied the charge that theirs was a party measure, and, seeking as much support as they could find, asked all to vote on the basis of their own convictions. Senator John Clayton told his colleagues:

> [He] was confident, that, in deciding the question, party feelings would have no place. He perfectly agreed with [Senator Dallas] that it should be solely a legislative business, and that they should act on it as such, and not suffer themselves to be carried away by any bias or prejudice whatever, or other feelings. It was a measure in which the interests of the whole American people were involved, and if . . . party feelings would have place, they

---

[175] (June 15, 16, 1840) *ibid.* 8 (appendix): p. 694.

[176] (March 17, 1832) Clay to Francis Brooke, *Clay Correspondence*, p. 329.

[177] (June 29, 1832) *ibid.* 1: p. 340.

[178] Remarks of Senator Benton. (May 26, 1832) *Register of Debates* 8: pp. 966–968.

[179] (June 12, 1832) *ibid.* 8: p. 3454.

[180] (May 26, 1832) *ibid.* 8: p. 975.

[181] (May 23, 1832) *ibid.* 8: p. 944.

[182] (June 1, 1832) *ibid.* 8: pp. 1000–1001.

[183] (June 6, 1832) *ibid.* 8: pp. 1046–1047.

[184] (June 8, 1832) *ibid.* 8: p. 1064.

would not be introduced by himself, or the friends with whom he generally coincided in sentiment.[185]

And even Senator Hugh Lawson White of Tennessee, not at this time affiliated with either side, "expressed himself as much pleased with the manner in which this important topic had been discussed throughout the period it had been before the Senate—in a manner that showed that no party had struggled for victory, but each and all for the public good."[186]

Clayton and White were both right, but so were Benton and Thomson. Only nine of the forty-eight Senators had been chosen by state legislatures at the time of the last presidential election, and had thus declared themselves in favor of Jackson or Adams. All nine remained loyal to the administration or the opposition, in accordance with their original commitment. Some of the other thirty-nine were undoubtedly swayed by debate. Continuously functioning parties did not exist in Congress in 1832. But others were known supporters of the administration or members of the so-called opposition. Senators Benton and Hill, though not chosen in 1828, were obvious Jacksonian stalwarts. Clay, the outstanding opposition leader, was elected to the Senate by the Kentucky legislature in 1831. Stray comments like Clayton's "the friends with whom he generally coincided in sentiment" suggest the existence of fairly distinctive groupings in Congress. Hill's and Benton's suggestion that the opposition party identified itself with the Bank of the United States at election time and then in Congress have some basis in fact.[187]

Even so, the President did not openly declare his intention of making renewal a party issue until he vetoed the bill passed by Congress in early July. Jackson's decision was not a surprise. As early as June 8, Hill told the Senate: "The friends of the President...have no fears for the results, if he shall do what they anticipate he will do."[188] On June 29 several days before final passage in the Senate, Clay wrote to a friend, "...If Jackson is to be believed, he will veto it."[189] Jackson's action did not induce a single senator to change his vote when the Senate sought passage over the veto. Six who originally supported the bill, did not vote on the second occasion, thus cutting the margin to three votes.[190]

1834

The bank issue most emphatically did become a party issue in the next session of Congress, however, and Jackson's important role in making it so is clearly revealed in his correspondence. He took an active interest in all the activities of Congress from the outset of the session. Committee assignments, the election of a speaker, strategy in both houses on the bank deposit issue, which dominated debate—all received presidential attention. As early as October 5, Jackson indicated his preoccupation with his administration's policy respecting the Bank of the United States. In his Annual Message, he wrote Van Buren, he would stress peace and prosperity and "then, the causes that led to the removal of the deposits with a forcible and in a concise manner, referring to the report of the Secretary of the Treasury. *This part must be well considered....*"[191] In early November, Senator Hugh Lawson White told the President that Vice-President Van Buren would not arrive in Washington until December 15. Van Buren had already agreed to have White, as President Pro-Tem, appoint the committees, whereas if the Vice-President had been present they would have had to be appointed by ballot. Jackson indicated his pleasure by writing to Van Buren that White was an ally and "I have no doubt will act *his part well*."[192] On November 30, the President wrote to the publisher of his party's Washington journal, Francis Blair, urging administration supporters in the House to rally round which ever candidate could win: either James Wayne of Georgia (who "will do nothing that will split the party") or Andrew Stevenson of Virginia (who "is true and faithful"). "There it is that noses ought to be counted."[193] Jackson reveals in this last remark an awareness that a portion of the House membership had to be wooed and did not identify with either the administration or the opposition. When the President became concerned about efforts by the opposition to restore the deposits, he wrote in anger to Van Buren, who was presiding over the Senate:

The opposition have everything to hope from delay, every engine of corruption is at work and our friends are indulging them with time to carry their corruption into effect. My d'r sir I am mortified at the game played by our friends. It is a time serving temporizing policy that destroys [all in favor of] it, and well calculated to loose that majority who would have been united by prompt, vigilant, and energetic measures at the commencement of the session.
If it is much longer postponed you may rest well assured that a panic will be introduced into Congress that will have the most pernicious effect. It will create a

[185] (May 26, 1832) *ibid.* 8: pp. 975–976.
[186] (June 7, 1832) *ibid.* 8: p. 1048.
[187] Bray Hammond, *Banks and Politics in America From the Revolution to the Civil War* (Princeton, paperback edition, 1967), pp. 385–386. Hammond's long and well-written study never focuses on banking as a party issue, which is certainly a flaw in this famous inquiry into the relationship between banking and politics.
[188] (June 8, 1832) *Register of Debates* 8: p. 1064.
[189] (June 29, 1832) Clay to Francis Brooke, *Clay Correspondence*, p. 340.
[190] *Register of Debates* 8: p. 1296.

[191] *Jackson Correspondence* 5: p. 217.
[192] (November 16, 1833) *ibid.* p. 226. White acted it, but not well enough: Administration supporters were outvoted 22 to 18 on an opposition motion to resume the appointment of committees by the Senate itself. (December 11, 1833) Clay to Francis Brooke, *Clay Correspondence*, p. 371.
[193] *Jackson Correspondence* 5: p. 230.

pretext for all those who are only confined by their pledge to their constituents, to vote for the restoration of the deposits, and may be the cause of giving two-thirds against my veto. Think of this and say to you friends how much has been, and how much may be lost by further delay in taking this question, and cease debate for the present and take the vote on the question.[194]

Clay, the most prominent of those opposed to Jackson, was also actively involved in all phases of congressional activity. On December 11, he indicated, in a note from the Senate chamber: "It would seem that the session opens with a majority in the House for the Administration, and a majority in the Senate against it. ... We hope," he added, "to reverse the majority in the House and to strengthen it in the Senate, *if we have no desertions* [italics added]."[195] On December 16:

We were highly gratified today in the Senate. We carried the appointment of every chairman of the committees as we wished. ... There is a fair prospect of our having in the Senate a majority of twenty-six or twenty-seven. ... I mean to open and push a vigorous campaign. ... I want aid—all the aid that can be given. I mean—which will surprise you—to be very prudent, but very resolute.[196]

On February 10:

The debate on the deposits continues. We are gaining both in public opinion and in number in the House of Representatives. We are probably still there in a minority. Although the majority is not large, and *will melt away if the current of public opinion continues to mix with us* [italics added].[197]

And, on March 23: "Things remain in *statu quo* here. There is a small, *but as yet inflexible majority*, sustaining the Executive in the House [italics added]."[198]

Clay here reveals both his continuing concern about the relative strength of the two parties in Congress and his rather accurate appraisal of that strength. The vote on the censure of Jackson, taken in June, was 29–16, only two or three votes different from his original estimate. But, what is also made quite plain in these hastily written notes is Clay's conviction that not everybody in Congress was committed to the concept of party loyalty, that debate and public opinion could sway votes.

Others indicated that not everyone considered the deposits question a party matter. Representative Samuel Moore of Virginia made the most succinct and direct statement among those who so argued.

[Moore] claimed the right to vote on this question, untrammeled by party, and with the single view of promoting what should appear to be for the best interests of the country, considering himself not so much the organ of the sentiments of any particular party as a representative of the whole people. Acting upon this principle, he would

vote, not upon the responsibility of any party, but upon his own, and for such measures as would be most conducive to the interests of those whom he had the honor to represent. ... .[199]

Representative Abel Huntington of New York, though elected as a Jackson supporter,

disclaimed altogether his being activated by private or political motives in this discussion, for it was a subject he felt to be far above such consideration, and he trusted that the House, in coming to a decision upon it, would not decide it as a mere party question, but as one affecting all the great interests of the country, which by their oaths they had bound themselves to maintain.[200]

Representative James Heath of Maryland, also elected as a supporter of the President, gave his approval to the views of those in Baltimore who presented a petition through him to the House, favoring restoration of the deposits, and added:

He came to this House not as a party man, but as an independent citizen; and he declared that no man in this nation had been a more pure, sincere and disinterested friend of General Jackson than himself, and that he had uniformly supported his measures. He appealed to the friends of the President on this floor to say whether, if the President should tomorrow send us a message informing us that he had directed the deposits to be restored, they would not give their hearty approbation and support to the measure.[201]

In the Senate, the utterances of Senator John Forsyth, a Jacksonian from Georgia, reveal the anguish endured by politicians who wished to be loyal to their party at the same time that they maintained their integrity and independence as a representative. When Clay called him "a firm supporter of the executive," Forsyth emphatically denied that he was "a defender of the executive, or of all his measures."[202] Earlier, Forsyth explained his course with the statement that

none of his acts emanated from any branch of this government, or that his support of any measure was given to it because it was an Administration measure. He had always done justice to every Administration, approving or condemning according to the dictates of his own judgment. And he felt that he ought to do the President the justice to say, that it was his ardent wish to do justice to the South as regarded the tariff.[203]

Later in the session he gave a rather ambiguous account of his position on the deposits question:

He had defended [removal], and his defence was before the world. He had said he would have delayed it. As a party man, he said he regretted there had not been more delay; but for the good of the country, perhaps the decision of the President was best.[204]

At another point in the debate Forsyth tangled

[194] (January 3, 1834) *ibid.* 5: pp. 238–239.
[195] Clay to Francis Brooke, *Clay Correspondence*, p. 371.
[196] Clay to Francis Brooke, *ibid.*, p. 375.
[197] Clay to Francis Brooke, *ibid.*, p. 377.
[198] Clay to Francis Brooke, *ibid.*, p. 383.

[199] (January 15, 1834) *Congressional Globe* 1: p. 106. Moore, incidentally, voted against the administration.
[200] (January 23, 1834) *ibid.* 1: p. 124.
[201] (February 18, 1834) *ibid.* 1: p. 182.
[202] (June 3, 1834) *ibid.* 1: p. 424.
[203] (January 23, 1834) *ibid.* 1: p. 127.
[204] (March 11, 1834) *ibid.* 1: p. 228.

with Senator Peleg Sprague of Maine, an Adams supporter when chosen in 1828. Sprague "protested against [the deposits issue] being made a mere party question," and added,

members had said they were elected as Jackson men, and therefore they had no discretion but to vote as Jackson men. He was not so situated. He owed no fealty to President Jackson; he was not elected as a Jacksonian. . . . He was elected to act on his convictions of duty, upon mature deliberation, upon such subjects as should come before him.[205]

Forsyth's response was to discount Sprague's protest against the deposit question's becoming a party measure, claiming Sprague had opposed the Jackson administration for four years. It would therefore be surprising if the Senator from Maine did not want the administration to be defeated. By contrast, Forsyth claimed he himself was "far above party" and had differed with most administrations since he had been in Congress, even the present one. Sprague then said he had to act for the best interests of his constituents, even if, as he knew, his political life would be sacrificed. The alternative would have been to seek his personal advancement by yielding his support to the administration and obtaining executive patronage. Unmoved, Forsyth coolly responded that talk of patronage by those out of power simply revealed their desire to get into power.[206]

Blair, the editor of the Washington Globe, sensed at the outset of the session the controversy over the government's bank deposits would turn into a full-fledged party struggle and punctuated his editorials from December onwards with accounts of opposition strategy, along with pleas for unity among administration supporters. Noting that the nullifiers and the "bank party" had joined in opposition to the President's removal policy, the Globe could not hide the fact that not all Jacksonians supported the President's action. Blair's device to induce unity was his somewhat specious argument that if one favored restoration of the deposits, he also favored rechartering the Bank:

Whatever, therefore, may HAVE BEEN THEIR OPINION UPON THE EXPEDIENCY OF REMOVAL, [Democrats] will go against restoration with an unbroken front. . . . The old chief will find an array of friends rallying around him. . . ., a united, firm, and zealous phalanx in both houses of Congress, whom money cannot not buy nor threats intimidate. There will be no longer room to doubt whether men are friends or enemies. For the time has come when all "those who are not for us are against us."[207]

Benton, not surprisingly, was the most direct and succinct in his assessment of the opposition. He told his Senate colleagues that the Bank of the United States and the opposition party were inextricably linked, indeed would succeed or fail together. Their objective was to defeat the President, as he was the major obstacle to recharter and thus their success.[208] Or, as the Globe put it: "The popularity of the President—his fortunate policy—his firm, uncompromising character, had left the nullifiers and bank leaders no means of compassing their respective purposes, but in the destruction of his influence. This has been the labor of the whole session."[209] Representative Balie Peyton of Tennessee, elected as a Clay partisan, inexplicably came out in opposition to those who combined against Jackson, and added to Benton's explanation:

Everyone must be aware that the present excitement against the President did not grow out of the removal of the deposits. That act was seized upon by the party leaders, to inflame the minds of the people, and to promote their chance of success in the deep game they were playing. The party was led by some of the highest order of talent, who were united by the common tie of disappointed ambition. One obstacle stood in the way—a man of stern integrity and inflexible patriotism stood as a pillar of the state. That pillar was to be overthrown, not by the removal of the deposits but by a continued and organized system of slander and abuse and agitation. All efforts were directed toward one object—to hold up the President as a tyrant, to resist whom will be patriotism.[210]

Others charged the opposition with deliberately creating excitement by means of contrived petitions, partisan speech-making at rallies which were packed with like-minded citizens, and even the misuse of the congressional franking privilege by loading certain districts with pro-bank literature.[211] The Globe even charged Clay with introducing a resolution which would have directed the executive to return the deposits to the Bank of the United States, not because the resolution would pass Congress, but because: "It is to enable the Bank attorneys in the Senate to make speeches in defence of their client, which the Bank printers in Washington will print by hundreds of thousands, and the Bank members of Congress will scatter over the whole country, under their franks."[212]

When opposition members in Congress began to call themselves "Whigs" in April during the debate over the deposits, Jackson stalwarts, such as Senators Grundy of Tennessee and Brown of North Carolina, objected to a label whose historic meaning was applicable to practically every politician in the country, to a label which was chosen as a cover term for "a union amongst discordant materials without the cement of any common principles to bind them together."[213]

---

[205] (April 17, 1834) ibid. 1: p. 318
[206] (March 11, 1834) ibid. 1: p. 228.
[207] Washington Globe, December 2, 1833.

[208] (April 17, 1834) Congressional Globe 1: p. 321.
[209] Washington Globe, May 5, 1834.
[210] (February 6, 1834) Congressional Globe 1: p. 159.
[211] (March 26, June 16, 1834) ibid. 1: pp. 267, 457.
[212] Washington Globe, May 29, 1834.
[213] (Brown: April 25, 1834; Grundy: May 1, 1834) Congressional Globe 1: pp. 345, 555–556. Also, Washington Globe, May 5, 1834.

In answer to the charge that the Bank of the United States and the new " Whig" party were allies, Representative George McDuffie, nullifier Democrat from South Carolina, insisted the President

had distributed the whole funds of the country among the local banks according to their political character. . . . The deposit banks had been selected expressly with a view to their party character, and the officers of those banks had already begun to figure in the political arena. . . . But now officers of the government were transformed into an army of electioneering agents.[214]

Senators Speleg Sprague of Maine, Thomas Ewing of Ohio, Theodore Frelinghuysen and Samuel Southard of New Jersey—all chosen as recognized opponents of Jackson—felt so strongly about the need for an alternative bank policy that they disobeyed the instructions of their legislatures and voted against the administration. Frelinghuysen was the only one who bothered to explain his course of action. He ignored his instructions, favoring instead petitions which expressed a contrary sentiment. When both were present he said he chose the more directly popular evidence. "By this he was willing to rise or fall, and he felt he should be sustained by his constituents."[215] When Democratic Senator Ether Shepley of Maine presented instructions passed by a large majority of both houses, adding, "I concur in all the opinions expressed," Sprague's response was to present petitions in opposition to the President's removal policy.[216] Shepley dismissed the use of petitions as a "new mode of electioneering," usually accompanied by "remarks of an electioneering tendency, and so avowed."[217] When Democratic Senator Thomas Morris presented instructions from Ohio's legislature, he later added petitions which also supported the President's policies. Ewing was silent, but disobeyed his instructions.[218] Sprague, as indicated above, tried to defend his position, even though it would end his career, which it did: he resigned in January, 1835.

During the course of the debate, various congressmen indicated their awareness of the great amount of public interest in the matter, and petitions poured in from all areas of the nation. Some senators methodically presented all such statements, both for and against the administration position, irrespective of what their own views were.[219] Others presented only those with which they were in agreement.[220] And

others defended "memorials" which favored their position as being nonpartisan and truly reflective of public opinion.[221] But several admitted the partisan character of the petitions they presented, arguing that public opinion had been accurately reflected nonetheless.[222] Well-known partisans, such as Senators Hill of New Hampshire and Brown of North Carolina presented documents contrary to their own position, but indicated the petitioners represented only a small minority of voters in their states.[223] Others, such as Senators Silas Wright of New York and Benjamin Leigh of Virginia, presented instructions from their state legislatures and quickly indicated their intention of supporting them.[224] In addition to the opposition senators listed above, only one administration senator —Rives of Virginia—disobeyed instructions, and he resigned.[225] That congressmen responded in various ways to petitions from their constituents is obvious. Seemingly all "memorials" were presented in the prescribed manner. Whether the work of party officials in certain localities or the spontaneous expression of the concern of particular economic or "citizen" groups, petitions suddenly and dramatically became a factor in determining how at least some congressmen voted on a major issue.

As the debate proceeded, the *Globe* became increasingly interested in the outcome, to the point that Blair did something he had never done before: he tried to predict the outcome. As early as February, the journal indicated a majority of twenty in the House of Representatives were against restoration of the government's deposits to the old Bank of the United States and a majority of fifty (including the nullifiers) were against renewal of the Bank's charter. On February 18, the House voted to submit the Secretary of the Treasury's letter, containing his reasons for having removed the deposits, to the Committee on Ways and Means, as the administration had desired, by a vote of 130–98.[226] On the following day, the *Globe* commented that the deposits would not be restored, that the previous day's vote had been decisive.[227] Somehow, Blair had learned that six Bank supporters voted with the friends of the administration in the 130–98 vote. On April 4, the House approved the Committee on Ways and Means' resolutions, the one that the Bank of the United States ought not to be rechartered by a majority of fifty-three (the *Globe*,

[214] (December 19, 1833) *Congressional Globe* **1**: p. 44.
[215] (January 27, 1834) *ibid*. **1**: p. 129.
[216] (February 3, April 30, 1834) *ibid*. **1**: pp. 146–147, 353.
[217] (February 3, 1834) *ibid*. **1**: pp. 146–147.
[218] (January 14, May 24, 1834) *ibid*. **1**: pp. 100, 385.
[219] (Senator Tyler of Virginia: March 13 and 17, 1834; Senators McKean and Wilkins of Pennsylvania: February 3, 11, 19, March 4, 14, April 4, June 3, 1834) *ibid*. **1**: pp. 235, 243, 147, 169, 186, 214, 237, 244, 421.
[220] (Representative Wilde of Georgia: March 5, 1834; Senator Knight of Rhode Island: February 17, May 9, June 18, 1834) *ibid*. **1**: pp. 217, 179, 374, 462.

[221] (Representative Selden of New York: February 3, 1834, Representative Hendricks of Indiana: May 26, 1834) *ibid*. **1**: pp. 149, 401.
[222] (Representatives Taylor and Clark of New York: May 5, 1834) *ibid*. **1**: pp. 367, 383–384.
[223] (Brown: February 11, 1834, Hill: February 17, 1834) *ibid*. **1**: pp. 169–170, 178–179.
[224] (Wright: January 30, 1834; Leigh: March 18, 1834; also, Representative Gordon of Virginia: March 3, 1834) *ibid*. **1**: pp. 136–138, 249, 212–213.
[225] (February 22, 1834) *ibid*. **1**: p. 193.
[226] *Ibid*. **1**: p. 186.
[227] *Washington Globe*, February 19, 1834.

over two months earlier had predicted a majority of fifty), the one that the deposits ought not to be restored by a majority of fifteen (the *Globe's* prediction: 16–20), the one that the deposit banks ought to be continued by a majority of thirteen (the *Globe* had not made a prediction on this resolution).[228] A few days later, the *Globe* even indicated how those who were absent on April 4 would have voted, had they been there.[229] What is extraordinary about all this is that for the first time in the Jacksonian period, Congress had been continuously and systematically examined as to the party loyalty of its members. That the *Globe* could have been so accurate is also important and is a tribute to the political perception of Jackson's chief editor.

More than perception was involved, however. Of the fourteen representatives who had clearly been elected as Jackson supporters but who opposed the administration's position on the deposits question, all but three either resigned or were defeated before the next session of the House.[230]

The editors of the opposition journal, *The National Intelligencer*, reacted with unusual bitterness to the administration victory, which the editors could explain only by reference to party pressure and the Democrats' avoidance of the real issue:

Had the question been propounded directly to the House, as indeed it of right ought to have been *are the reasons of the Secretary of the Treasury sufficient to justify the removal of the public deposits from the Bank of the United States?*—it is probable that a large number would have been found to resist the influence of party, and boldly and independently to have answered *NO.* Artfully avoiding that proper issue, the party managers presented a different question to the House, and obtained a show of support for the President, by an oblique and collateral question, which would probably have been withheld on a direct one.[231]

As to party influence:

It appears . . . that more than a third of the whole number of affirmative votes was given by *two* states, one of which furnishes the President, and the other the Vice President of the United States; and it cannot be doubted, that the . . . votes of these two states [are] attributable to the political connexion of these two high officers of the government, rather than to any identity of sentiment on the question among the people of those two states. In a word, New York politics has controlled the decision.

The interests of party have prevailed over the interests of the country. There is not the smallest doubt, that a majority of the House of Representatives disapproved of the removal of the deposits. . . . Is it not lamentable that, yet so remote, intrigue and cabals connected with the next Presidential election should already control legislation upon the great interests of the country.[232]

The *Intelligencer's* account of what happened and why is itself partisan and therefore only partially accurate. It is true that twenty-eight New York Democrats voted with the administration (with three not voting), but it is also true that all known opposition members from the state (eight in number) voted against the resolutions. In Tennessee, the situation was different and perhaps justified the *Intelligencer's* explanation. Every member of the thirteen-man delegation, except one, supported Jackson, even though it contained five opposition representatives. Only Davy Crockett withstood what must have been pressure on the whole delegation to unite behind the man who, as President, had made the deposits question the supreme test of political and personal loyalty to him.

Jackson was quite obviously happy over the outcome of the House voting on April 6: "The overthrow of the opposition in the House of Representatives... was a triumphant one, and puts to death that mammoth of corruption and power, the Bank of the United States....[233] I have obtained a glorious triumph over the opposition. . . ."[234]

But both Jackson and Blair were furious about Clay's successful Senate motion of censure for the manner in which the President removed the deposits. Blair, who had attacked throughout the session a number of opposition senators for disobeying the instructions of their legislatures,[235] was convinced the censure resolution would have failed if the senators had supported the President as they had been instructed to do.[236] The *Globe* listed Senators Sprague of Maine, Bell of New Hampshire, Frelinghuysen and Southard of New Jersey, Ewing of Ohio, Mangum of North Carolina, and both Black and Poindexter of Mississippi as the opponents of the administration who disobeyed instructions. Jackson added, after the final vote of 29–16 in favor of the resolutions was recorded in early June, that those senators "who have violated their pledges, and are acting in open violation of the instructions of their constituents" would be defeated and that the next Senate would have "a virtuous majority."[237] Whether or not the instructed senators should have felt their legislature's command

---

[228] *Ibid.,* April 5, 1834. *Congressional Globe* 1: p. 292.
[229] *Washington Globe,* April 8, 1834.
[230] Selden of New York resigned. King of Pennsylvania resigned. Bell of Ohio was defeated. Duncan of Illinois became governor of the state later in the year. Heath and Turner of Maryland were defeated. Gholson of Virginia resigned; Gordon was defeated. Rencher of North Carolina resigned, but not until 1839. Felder of South Carolina resigned; and so did Pinckney, but not until 1837. Foster of Georgia was defeated. Thomas of Louisiana resigned. This information, as well as that involving party affiliation generally, was garnered from the *Biographical Directory of the American Congress, 1774–1961* (Washington, 1961).
[231] *National Intelligencer,* April 7, 1834.

[232] *Ibid.*
[233] (April 6, 1834) Jackson to Andrew Jackson, Jr., *Jackson Correspondence* 5: p. 259.
[234] (April 6, 1834) Jackson to John Coffee, *ibid.* 5: p. 260.
[235] *Washington Globe,* January 31, February 22, March 1, 1834.
[236] *Ibid.,* March 31, 1834.
[237] (June (?), 1834) Jackson to Edward Livingston, *Jackson Correspondence* 5: p. 272.

extended to a proposal involving the censure of the President is at least debatable. What was not was the clear majority of the opposition in the Senate during the 1833–1834 session. Only one senator elected as a Democrat since 1829 voted with that opposition.[238] As for those senators who disobeyed their instructions, the outcome was hardly in the form of the purge which Jackson hoped for. Sprague resigned in January, 1835; Bell retired in 1835; Frelinghuysen also retired in 1835, but Southard continued in office for years; Ewing served out his term, but was defeated when he sought reelection in 1837; Mangum later resigned, in November, 1836; Poindexter retired in 1835, but Black remained a senator until 1838.

The deposits question of 1834 had thus created a congressional division based upon a far deeper recognition of party loyalty than had any previous matter considered by Congress. It was during the debates on the deposits, in fact, that opposition congressmen attained a level of self-awareness sufficient for them to think of a name for themselves. The "Whigs" were "in opposition" to "King Andrew I," and, like the Republicans of the 1790's, were thus united about what they did not want and not about what they wanted, something which would shape their destiny throughout most of their brief, twenty-year history. Never again, after the spring of 1834, would Congress adjourn without talk of "party strength" and "party issues." It was always thereafter a matter of concern whether a party might make something of a divisive nature a further test of party loyalty.

1835–1837

The short-term impact of the deposits controversy was to create an opposition party in the South. Van Buren's presidential candidacy in 1836 made the division a lasting one. Jackson thought the Democratic split on the South, which by 1835 had assumed the form of support for Hugh Lawson White of Tennessee as the party's candidate, was "truly mortifying," since a group of politicians who had supported him were attempting to destroy the party "by diverting a portion of the Republican strength." It must have been particularly galling to Jackson to conclude that White, an old friend, had probably been persuaded by Bell—also an erstwhile supporter— "who threw himself upon the opposition" during the contest for Speaker in the House during June, 1834. The President calculated that the entire opposition plus twenty administration supporters "whom [Bell] induced to believe, that he would remain true to the party" gave Bell his victory.[239]

The presidential campaign of 1836 had the effect of diverting the attention of leading party politicians from their division over the banking issue to a concern for victory in the election itself. The Jacksonians, unable to reunite after the defections of 1834, rallied round Van Buren's candidacy, stressing the fact that he was Jackson's personal choice. The Whigs, unable to settle on a single candidate, supported regional ones and stressed their opposition to executive encroachments.

Van Buren's narrow political victory produced a prompt political response. No less a figure than Henry Clay, by this time the recognized leader of the opposition in the Senate, gave expression to what Whigs thought would be their strategy at the outset of Van Buren's presidency. Clay—as always—believed the Whigs should unite in support of his "American System," but added:

Undoubtedly, such an opposition should [also] avail itself of the errors of the new Administration; but it seems to me that it would acquire greater force by availing itself also of that fatal error in its origins, which resulted from the President-elect being the designated successor of the present incumbent. If a President may name his successor, and bring the whole machinery of government, including its one hundred thousand dependents into the canvass, and if by such means he achieves a victory, such a fatal precedent as this must be rebuked and reversed, or there is an end of the freedom of election. No one doubts that this has been done. And . . . it will again be attempted, and unless corrected by the people, it will become, in time, the established practice of the country. Now, I think that no wisdom or benefit, in the measures of the new Administration, can compensate or atone for this vice in its origins. Still, this point may be pressed or not, according to circumstances, in different states.[240]

Clay was probably sincere. But he also could not pass up the opportunity to attack the Democrats in the same way that he had been attacked in 1825 and thereafter. In any case, the Whigs—while in Congress—did not press the point.

Democrats sensed what the true basis of Whig unity was. Indeed a long-time political aid of the President wondered whether the Democracy could survive such political cohesion unless it too was united:

Our party seems to be battling on the very brink of a dangerous precipice and unless we continue united we must fall over. Divisions in our ranks, more especially among our chieftains, will lead to inevitable destruction. . . . Our adversaries, at least, give us an example worthy of imitation—differing fundamentally in their principles—here a Nullifier and there a consolidationist—

---

[238] John King of Georgia, who later—in 1837—resigned. *Congressional Globe* 1: pp. 424–426.

[239] (April 24, 1835) Jackson to J. C. Guild, *Jackson Correspondence* 5: pp. 338–339. That the administration had assumed Bell, upon his electon as speaker, would support it is indicated by the following editorial which appeared in the *Globe* after Bell's

election: "[Bell] has given a uniform, able, and consistent support to all [the President's] measures. He is a man of fine genious, high attainments, and distinguished for his eloquence." *Washington Globe*, June 2, 1834. Jackson's assessment of the vote obviously came after Bell's defection, which either indicates he was not well-informed on the nature of the voting on the speakership at the end of the 1833–1834 session, or—what is far more likely—he interpreted the vote to suit his purposes.

[240] (December 19, 1836) Clay to Francis Brooks, *Clay Correspondence*, p. 409.

here a high tariffite and there a free trade man—Yet do they keep in close phalanx as a party to overthrow the existing Administration, and unless we stand shoulder to shoulder in resisting them, victory will assuredly perch on their banner. When they once get into power they may wrangle among themselves, but shall we, as a party, ever again be enabled to rally and to subdue them? Never.[241]

The depression which began about the time Van Buren assumed office led the new President to call a special session of Congress to approve of a measure which he believed was necessary to the future prosperity of the nation: the complete separation of government revenue from the banking system and the establishment of an independent treasury system to store those revenues. In his Message, the President indicated that the depression was caused by speculation and an overextension of credit which had led to a suspension of specie payments by state banks. Rejecting the alternative of a new Bank of the United States as "repulsive" to public opinion, Van Buren selected a policy which plainly contradicted Jackson's. But though a reversal, the new proposal was presented as a party measure with as much vigor as Jackson had displayed in making his actions respecting bank deposits the first great test of party loyalty. Van Buren did not bother to excuse the contradiction except to say that the deposit bank "performed with fidelity and without any embarrassment to themselves or to the community their engagements to the Government. . . . "[242] The President concluded, however, that the experience the nation had when government deposits were left in state banks was such that private investors controlled public money and used it to extend credit without proper caution.[243]

Van Buren thus staked out the basic objective of his administration at the outset of his term in office. The fact that the opposition was equally committed to the creation of a new Bank of the United States meant that the major test of party loyalty would again be one's position on banking policy.

Even so, the *Intelligencer* denied that "the bank question" had been or should become a party question[244] and was delighted whenever a Democrat, such as Senator King of Georgia, spoke out against the administration position,[245] which suggests that the editors were in fact more concerned about encouraging Democratic defections than in keeping party politics out of Congress. More convincingly, the journal argued the Whigs did not simply advocate a new national bank, but sought "to recover for the legislature the powers usurped from it by the executive, to rescue from the executive grasp and absolute possession the money of the people."[246]

Blair, in his *Globe*, also urged that the bank issue be removed from party politics. Just as the President's proposal would separate the government's financial activities from the banking system, so too should the banking and other economic interests separate themselves from politics. Only when this occurred would the economy recover:

The question of the bank has drawn every interest associated with it into politics. . . . [Everyone should be] desirous of separating the pecuniary interests of individuals and corporations from the results of party conflicts. All must be anxious that the standard of value shall cease to be a subject of party conflict. . . . Confidence will instantly spring up when the currency ceases to be a subject of party warfare, and quiet industry will then soon redeem all classes from the thralldom in which the political strife has involved them. [The economy will not recover] while two great political parties make these pecuniary questions the principal issues to be contested in their conflicts.[247]

And yet *one* day later, Blair revealed the basic ambiguity of his position on party politics in a manner more blatant than anything his rival editors managed to offer.

The consummating measure . . . will . . . pass, if it be not prevented by the procrastinating artifices of the opposition. They cannot succeed at their posts until the close of the week. Such is the patriotic feeling which animates the Democracy at this moment that we do not believe their vigilance will sleep by night or by day. Even some who hesitated on this all-absorbing question, are now sensible that the public will demand it.[248]

A pep talk about closing ranks and standing firm and staying united is hardly compatible with a plea that the banking issue be removed from party politics.

When the independent treasury bill was introduced, it quickly became apparent most members of both houses of Congress would support the position taken by their respective parties. Several of those who decided not to felt obliged to explain their deviancy, which was the best possible evidence of party pressure.

In the Senate, where the Democrats had a sizable majority, six administration supporters defected, with another five abstaining. Senator Tallmadge of New York, a leader of the conservatives, whose opposition on this issue was the basis for a permanent split, emphasized what a number of others referred to. The President's scheme had actually been introduced by a Whig congressman from Georgia in 1835. At that time the Jackson administration had opposed the measure, and so had Tallmadge. Jackson then persuaded his party to support his deposit system, and so had Tallmadge. Since that time, however, the Van Buren administration had concluded that the deposit system had failed and supported a scheme the Democratic party had scorned two years before. But Tallmadge still believed the deposit system was

---

[241] August 5, 1837, John Brockenbrough to Van Buren, Van Buren Papers, second series, Library of Congress.
[242] Richardson, editor, *Messages and Papers* 4: p. 1548.
[243] *Ibid.*, pp. 1550–1552.
[244] *National Intelligencer*, September 25, 1837.
[245] *Ibid.*
[246] *Ibid.*, September 11, 1837.

[247] *Washington Globe*, September 27, October 10, 1837.
[248] *Ibid.*, October 11, 1837.

the most effective one. He argued Jackson's specie circular—which would have been rejected if Congress had had the opportunity to vote on it—caused the financial crisis of 1837. An independent treasury system, if adopted, would ruin the whole credit structure of the country, ultimately undermining the state banks themselves.[249] Senator King of Georgia wanted the bill delayed so that his constituents could consider the proposition properly. Though he had supported Van Buren in the 1836 election, King thought it was his duty as a senator to give "his free, unbiassed opinion." The Georgian wished the President had "taken the trouble to make himself more acquainted with the facts in the case." King thought Van Buren's explanation of the depression was wrong. Like Tallmadge, King pointed to the specie circular as the major cause. In fact, the President's "whole message appears to him to be made up from stump speeches, paragraphs of editors of newspapers, and *saws* from hack politicians. . . . He had found it necessary to take a stand against executive encroachments, and wanted his friends to rally [around] him."[250] Senator Tipton of Indiana asserted that the whole thrust of Democratic banking policies had led directly to the recession. As for the present bill, "he would not declare in advance that he would not go for it, or for something like it, but he would be slow in yielding his support, and he hoped that a better remedy would be found." So far, he tended to favor a simple extension of the deposit system.[251] Senator Preston of South Carolina, who abstained, also traced the economic depression to the executives' policies on banking. He expressed his horror over the growth of presidential power and vowed to oppose any measure which would increase it.[252]

When, on October 2, the Senate defeated motions by Preston and Rives (of Virginia) to continue the state deposit system by a vote of 26–22 and went on to engross the administration's bill, 25–23, Blair wrote in the *Globe* that since "*four* friends of the Administration [were absent]. . . . it may be considered certain that the bill will pass the Senate."[253] The final vote, taken on October 3, was 26–20 in favor of the measure. Of the five who abstained, the *Globe* believed Cuthbert of Georgia and Mouton of Louisiana "would have supported the measure," but had been absent throughout the session.[254] Parker and Rives of Virginia and Preston of South Carolina also abstained, probably in every case because of disagreement with the administration position. Joining King, Tipton, and Tallmadge in outright opposition

were Black of Mississippi, Nicholas of Louisiana, and McKean of Pennsylvania.[255]

As in the Senate, some of the Democrats in the House who defected offered an explanation for their action. Clark of New York told his colleagues on the day they voted that "the subject matter of this bill is one on which there is, among the friends of the Administration, a difference of opinion, and, I have no doubt, an honest difference." Clark supported the motion introduced shortly before he spoke to lay the bill on the table. He did so in order that his constituents could be asked for their opinion. As an administration measure the independent treasury scheme was new, and public opinion had not been adequately formed. In Clark's own state, even the *Albany Argus*, "a journal which possesses great influence over the country press," had not expressed its views before the beginning of the present session. Clark said he always deferred to the will of his constituents, "when formed upon reflection and deliberation, and fairly and fully expressed." He thought the government could wait a while, as it had carried on its fiscal operations satisfactorily since the banks had suspended specie payments. Clark had not proper contact with his constituents, as had most members of the House, since April, because of "pressing business."[256] It is difficult to determine how many Clark spoke for. He was, however, the only Democrat in the large New York delegation to desert the President.

Mason of Virginia confessed that he disagreed with administration:

It is with the utmost reluctance that I am now brought to differ with those with whom I have heretofore acted. . . . This difference, however, I am pleased to consider, is at least but one of mere expediency and in itself contains nothing which should sever those who are united otherwise in the preservation and support of those great and leading principles which activate political parties. . . . Differences of opinion necessarily pertain to deliberation; it is against the constitution of our nature that it should be otherwise; intelligence, reason, and sound judgment, are alike hostile to entire unanimity, nor would our representative government be anything more than a mere formal acquiescence in the will of some ordained superior; if the doctrine were allowed to hold, that party discipline exacts an unconsidered sanction to every measure, which brings a recommendation from the Executive chair. . . . Such is certainly not the spirit of our institutions; nor should it be the spirit of any party that would act safely and wisely, or even successfully, in the administration of government committed to their charge.[257]

Though Mason was disingenuous when he asserted that his difference with the administration was one of "mere expediency," what followed, nevertheless, was perhaps the most perceptive statement of the decade

---

[249] (September 22, 1837) *Congressional Globe* 5: pp. 53–54.
[250] (September 23, 1837) *ibid.* 5: pp. 60–61.
[251] (September 23, 1837) *ibid.* 5: pp. 61–62.
[252] (September 30, 1837) *ibid.* 5 (appendix): pp. 296–297.
[253] *Washington Globe*, October 3, 1837.
[254] *Ibid.*, October 4, 1837.

[255] *Congressional Globe* 5: p. 100.
[256] (October 14, 1837) *ibid.* 5: pp. 140–141.
[257] (October 11, 1837) *ibid.* 5 (appendix): p. 214.

on the proper limits of party loyalty made by any politician who thought of himself as a "party man."

Garland, another Virginian, apparently was regarded as the leader of renegade group in his state's delegation, which produced five, the largest number of defectors. Obviously upset by the charges levied against him and his friends by the Democratic press, the Virginian scoffed at the accusations that he and the others were traitors to their party and that he was, in effect, the head of a new party. The Democratic Party, he asserted, had betrayed itself by supporting a measure it had denounced a scant two years before. Garland had maintained the original Democratic position; the Van Buren administration had changed, not Garland.[258]

By contrast only two who were elected as Whigs adopted a position contrary to their party's. And of these, Robertson of Virginia, claimed: "I have never so far enlisted under the banners of either [party] as to give up the exercise of my own judgment, nor consented to submit to the dictation of any party, or of any man in this house—or in the White House." Having decided as early as 1834 that he favored the complete separation of banking and government, Robertson simply maintained that position. Noting that Democrats had changed their minds since then, he added: "It is not for me to question the sincerity of either party; that is between them and their consciences. We have to do here with measures, not motives. I think now as I thought then; and will not change my course, because the Administration party, or the opposition party, may think fit to change theirs."[259] Representative Pope of Kentucky, though originally elected as a Jackson supporter, told the electors of his district in the previous campaign "with openness and candor" (in his own words) that he believed the Bank of the United States was "necessary and proper" both as a fiscal agent of the government and as a regulator of the paper-money system. Pope thus had "appealed to no party on party grounds," had avoided the "mere party struggles" of the country, and proceeded to declare his opposition to the independent treasury bill.[260]

Even those who voted the party line were occasionally anxious to explain their action beforehand with reference to considerations entirely apart from party. As Pickens of South Carolina put it:

I never stop to inquire who may be with me, or who may be against me on a question of that character. All I ask myself is, is it a constitutional proposition, and if it be right and correct to maintain it. . . . The mere triumphs of party I disregard, I throw aside party considerations where a great question is concerned. . . . On such a question . . . I subscribe to no party creed.[261]

Everyone knew the vote would be close; no one predicted the outcome with any confidence. Even the *Globe* and the *Intelligencer*, in their editorials, were uncertain. Blair, in fact, was quite jittery and anxious. On October 4 (after the Senate vote): "So far as the House has given indications of its feelings by legislation, there is good ground to hope that it will sustain the other branches of the government." On October 11: "We learn from our correspondents that the final vote is looked for with intense anxiety; and every intermediate step is scrutinized with the utmost solicitude as an indication of the result." On October 12, two days before the final vote: "What will the country say if, after the strong and unequivocal expression of its will . . . , the all important question should be defeated by chicane." Apparently this anxiety was not shared by those who viewed the scene from afar, perhaps not even by the President himself. An old political friend of Van Buren wrote shortly before the House acted: "[Having observed the activities of the Congressional session,] I trust nothing will prevent the passage at this session of the sub-treasury bill now before the House."[262]

The House vote of October 14, 1837, was on Clarke of New York's motion to table the bill. The motion carried 120–107.[263] Though obviously distressed, Blair nonetheless wrote a long editorial later that same day in which he explained, from a Democratic perspective, what had happened. Clarke's intention was not to defeat the measure, but to postpone it, so that he could consult with his constituents. "This appeal was successful with some ten or a dozen of the Democratic members, and the whole opposition uniting with them in a body." Blair here is disturbingly imprecise. Actually two Whigs and twenty-one Democrats broke ranks. The only major defection, as already indicated, was in the Virginia delegation, where there were five renegade Democrats. The other fourteen were from North Carolina (3), South Carolina (3), Illinois (3), Ohio (2), Kentucky, New York, Massachusetts, Maine, and New Hampshire. Blair was obviously more concerned about minimizing the defections than in striving for complete accuracy. Nevertheless, he argued that "if the privileged question to lay the bill on the table had not prevailed, the bill would have been carried by a majority [as was ascertained by the declaration of several members who voted for the postponement] of *three votes*." Perhaps, but Blair's flat assertion that this would have been the case is not totally convincing. He went on:

We were sure that the Federal party would unite with any portion of the less resolved of the Democratic members, to parry a decision on the issue proposed in the Message. The motive which influenced the few Republicans in

---

[258] (September 25, 1837) *ibid.* 5: p. 202.
[259] (October 11, 1837) *ibid.* 5 (appendix): pp. 133–134.
[260] (October 12, 1837) *ibid.* 5: p. 306.
[261] (October 10, 1837) *ibid.* 5 (appendix): p. 179.

[262] October 12, 1837, E. Throope to Van Buren, Van Buren Papers, second series, Library of Congress.
[263] *Congressional Globe* 5: p. 141.

regard to laying over the bill, did not influence the federal party. They were prepared to vote against the measure and every other that did not comprehend a national bank.

Blair was convinced that it was simply a matter of time before the independent treasury system would be enacted into law: "Never before has a measure of such magnitude, and having such important bearings upon the political as well as pecuniary relations of the country made such rapid progress in conciliating public opinion." The Whigs, he argued, had resorted and would continue to resort to an expedient to defeat the President's proposal. But, "the great body of the Republicans knew full well that their constituents wished a divorce of government and politics from the money power of the banks; and nobly did their duty. They will receive the applause of their constituents when they meet them."[264]

Two days later, the *Intelligencer* commented on the House vote. The majority of thirteen the journal's editors thought was

a large majority, considering the composition of the House, and the efforts which were made by the leaders of the "party" to force it through Congress. Thus have the representatives of the people triumphantly borne us out in the prediction . . . that the [members of the House] would be found, like true patriots, acting honestly, independently, and without subservience to the executive's wishes.[265]

The *Globe's* reaction was immediate. Now asserting that six out of the eleven Democrats who voted for postponement did so in order to check with their constituents, Blair added:

[The motive of the *Intelligencer's* editors] is sufficiently obvious. [That journal] hopes to array against the members who voted with the opposition *for delay*, the hostility of every republican in their respective districts, and by driving from such representatives their original friends, to drive them into the embraces of federalism. Some of the gentlemen concerned, we know, appreciate this sinister policy properly.[266]

1837–1838

In the aftermath of legislative defeat, the Democrats suffered electoral losses as well in the state elections which took place in a time of continuing economic depression. A close political associate of the President, Representative Cambreleng of New York, expressed both the dismay and the hope of loyal Democratic Congressmen at this particular juncture when he wrote:

We are beaten here [in New York] and elsewhere—so much for our party's surrendering our principles in the last legislature.—The Conservatives have everywhere openly united with the Whigs. . . . We have now got

rid of the traitors and are prepared for a fresh start. We must once in ten years be whipped into our principles."[267]

The "fresh start" came when Senator Silas Wright of New York, another old political ally of the President, immediately reintroduced the independent treasury proposal at the outset of the next session. What became quickly evident was that for the first time every member of Congress would be regarded primarily as a Democrat or a Whig, either as a loyal party man or as a renegade. Conspicuously absent from the accounts of the proceedings in both the *Globe* and the *Intelligencer* were pleas for politicians to rise above the status of partisan, though congressional leaders of both sides were, of course, delighted when they learned of defections from the ranks of their opponents. All congressmen had talked to their constituents about the matter. Several legislatures had instructed their senators, and most obeyed, something the *Globe* favored on principle, even when the instructions were to oppose the administration.[268] No longer could anyone urge delay on the grounds his constituents were uninformed. The 1837–1838 session of Congress thus contained the first total party conflict of the second-party era.

On February 5, the *Globe* produced an editorial which revealed with clarity the extent to which it was now able to link party with issue. Such a commentary could not have been written three or four years earlier, dramatic evidence of the emergence of party in Congress:

In the course of our experience, we have never known a public question in respect to which there existed through the Democratic ranks such universal accord of opinion, as there does at this moment upon this very point. How the public money should be kept, and what kind of funds shall be receivable for public dues, are questions in respect to which some diversity of sentiment has exhibited itself; but in respect to the inexpediency of restoring the use of the public money to the banks (with the exception of a few individuals, who, it is well known, have gone over, *body and soul* to the Opposition), there is but one voice and one mind among all claiming to be Democrats. If there is a single press from Maine to Georgia, or throughout the valley of the Mississippi, which is honestly regarded . . . as an exponent of the Democratic members of the legislature of any state, or the mass of the unbought and unsophisticated Democracy in any quarter of the Union, hold a different opinion, we are not aware of it. . . . We are persuaded that we speak within bounds when we say, that of the members of Congress who profess to adhere to the Democratic Party, there are not a dozen to be found who will support it.[269]

Even the President commented more openly than either he or Jackson had before on the prospects of a major legislative proposal. On March 2, in the midst of the debate over the revivified independent treasury

[264] *Washington Globe*, October 14, 1837.
[265] *National Intelligencer*, October 16, 1837.
[266] *Washington Globe*, October 16, 1837.

[267] November 9, 1837; C. C. Cambreleng to Van Buren, Van Buren Papers, second series, Library of Congress.
[268] *Washington Globe*, March 1, 1838.
[269] *Ibid.*, February 5, 1838.

bill, he wrote to Jackson: "[Mr. Wright's bill] will pass the Senate and I hope the House, but the latter is far from certain."[270] On March 17: "We are not yet out of the woods with our independent treasury bill, but hope for the best. Of its passage in the Senate there is no doubt, though it may be by the casting vote of the Vice President."[271] Van Buren even got quite specific, indicating reasons why particular Democrats could or could not support his measure:

Morris [of Ohio] cannot vote for it because it permits paper to be rec[eive]d to any extent, and our friend Cuthbert [of Georgia] because the permission to do so is not more general. The debate continues to be carried on in the Senate with unabated earnestness. . . .
Our friends Brown [of North Carolina] and Strange [of North Carolina] have done themselves high honor by their speeches in the Senate which are scarcely inferior to the best that have been delivered. Col. Benton is now making one which promises to be of the very first order. I presume they (B & S) have sent you copies.[272]

Actually, the final version of the bill satisfied both Morris and Cuthbert, and they voted for it. Whether they were also in any sense pressured by the President or his closest Senate allies cannot be determined. Van Buren's comments suggest he felt he had to accept a Democratic senator's opposition whenever it was firmly expressed.

At first Clay wanted action on the measure delayed because most legislatures which either had or might be induced to instruct their senators had Whig majorities who could instruct Democratic senators.[273] But by mid-February he shifted his strategy. State elections since the special session had, as already indicated, resulted in the reduction or obliteration of Democratic majorities. Clay drew the conclusion that the administration measure had, in effect, already been repudiated in these elections. He then issued this clarion call:

I call upon all the Senators; let us bury, deep and forever, the character of the partisan, rise up patriots and statesmen, break the vile chains of party, throw the fragments to the winds, and fell the proud satisfaction that we have made but a small sacrifice to the paramount obligations which we owe our common country.[274]

Even though the plea had little impact, Clay refrained from estimating the relative strength of the parties his rhetoric had failed to demolish. Nose counting was something he had done rather inaccurately during the special session, when he predicted the House favored rechartering the Bank of the United States.[275]

---

[270] March 2, 1838, Van Buren to Jackson, Van Buren Papers, second series, Library of Congress.
[271] March 17, 1838, *Ibid.*
[272] *Ibid.*
[273] (January 16, 31, 1838) *Congressional Globe* 6: pp. 112, 151. Clay, of course, did not use these words, but his inference was clear.
[274] (February 19, 1838) *ibid.* 6 (appendix): p. 619.
[275] *Washington Globe*, September 25, 26, October 5, 1837.

The *Intelligencer* also refrained, admitting throughout the weeks of the debate that the votes would be close. On February 19:

"We are asked almost every day, "will the subtreasury project pass?" We cannot tell. . . . One can more easily read the signs of the times than penetrate the designs of the "party." [On March 15, a rare prediction, and an inaccurate one:] "From our impression of the state of feeling and opinion prevailing in and about the capitol yesterday, we really entertain a belief that the subtreasury bill, which has been so much debated in the Senate, is not likely to become law, without very material alterations.

On June 9th, the *Intelligencer* accepted the report of the Washington correspondent of the *New York Courier* who had written that a small majority in the House was opposed to the administration measure, "but a majority so small that it is believed every member must be at his post to ensure its defeat." The journal urged all representatives to "be responsible" and to "do their duty." On June 13: Though many papers printed detailed calculations of the outcome of the vote in the House, "for ourselves, we were never skillful at what is called counting noses, and we cannot, therefore, answer for the accuracy of any of these reckonings." On June 21, the *Intelligencer* urged Whigs to respect the Democratic "conservatives" who were dividing their party—who had been Jacksonians, but who could no longer support that party. They were honest men who should be welcomed as allies against a common foe. Together Whigs and "conservatives" could win. Quite frankly, the "conservatives" held the balance of power, and their support would result in the administration's defeat.

Two days later, on June 23, the Whig journal indicated it was regrettable the independent treasury bill had been forced on the House so late in the session. "Sturdy resistance" and "probable defeat" were justified and should have been expected. The scheme, if adopted, would have been the "entering wedge of perpetual party domination." It would have been a "real barbarity" to have forced the bill through the House, even if a majority had favored it. The House should have been giving its attention to measures that had matured through debate. In this way the *Intelligencer* provided a response which was appropriate either to passage or to rejection. Such a response makes sense only if one accepts the proposition that the leading Whig journal did not know what the result would be and was quite apprehensive.

Actually, nothing turned out exactly the way Van Buren, Clay, the *Globe*, or the *Intelligencer* hoped it would. But the continued involvement of political and journalistic leaders with a major issue as it pertained to the parties in Congress was itself of major significance.

Not all Democratic senators obeyed their instructions. Grundy of Tennessee and both Buchanan and McKean of Pennsylvania did.[276] Wall of New Jersey, Niles of Connecticut, and Morris of Ohio did not,[277] either because they felt their instructions were ambiguous, in the case of Niles, or because the legislature which had elected them had a different opinion on the measure than the later legislature which instructed them.

Calhoun supported the independent treasury scheme as being in keeping with his state-rights principles,[278] but when the Senate voted against his proposal, which would have required specie in the payment of all public debts, a scheme which would have been phased in over a period of time, he voted against the Senate sub-treasury bill shorn of his proposal.[279] Calhoun's colleague, Senator Preston from South Carolina, also voted against the measure. In a brief speech he referred to Van Buren's as a "bungling administration" and suggested the Senate ought to have passed the independent treasury scheme and let the administration demonstrate how bad its proposed system would have been. But, upon reflection, he concluded such a political move would be too injurious to the nation's welfare. It is difficult to determine whether Preston was opposed to the independent treasury system generally, or, following Calhoun's lead, just to its operation without his colleague's specie payment amendment. His intemperate language suggests the former.[280]

Tallmadge of New York and Rives of Virginia personified the "conservative" revolt against the administration and, of course, opposed the bill. During the debates, Wright and Tallmadge exchanged comments which illustrated the nature of the division. Wright asserted his loyalty to the Democratic party, under both Jackson's and Van Buren's leadership, and to its measures. The opposition to both presidents had involved the same politicians. Thus Wright was an orthodox Democrat. But Tallmadge argued that, while it was true Wright had been loyal to both presidents, the measures they favored were erratic and inconsistent. To Tallmadge and Rives, a policy which favored a state deposit bank system for government revenue was totally antithetical to a policy which would lead to the creation of a sub-treasury system. They happened to prefer the former, which was Jackson's party's original proposal. The inference was that orthodoxy should pertain to consistency and loyalty with respect to measures, not just men. Tallmadge added: "[Wright] has been guided by the executive index; as it had pointed in its revolutions around the political circle, so followed

his colleague; and he must take care . . . lest, in his wanderings, he should be lost like the twelve tribes in the desert."[281]

There were three dissident Democrats in the Senate whose opposition can not be clearly explained: Robert Nicholas of Louisiana, John Ruggles of Maine, and John Tipton of Indiana. All were elected Democrats; none explained his position during the debate; none was instructed to vote against the independent treasury bill.

In the special session of the previous fall six Democratic senators had voted against the independent treasury scheme, and five did not vote. In the second vote, taken on March 26, 1836, all senators participated, with the result that nine Democrats opposed the bill. Of these, three were instructed to do so. And so, as far as the Senate was concerned, there were still a half dozen Democrats unwilling to support the administration. If Van Buren sought to bring any direct pressure to bear on the recalcitrant members of his own party, it is not in evidence. And if he did, he failed. In any case, a united Whig contingent, even with six Democratic renegades, was not sufficient to defeat the administration's proposal. It passed by the narrowest of margins: 27–25.[282]

In the house, the vote on passage, on June 25, was 111–125 against the measure. Eighteen representatives elected as Democrats failed to support the President. Their defection alone produced the result which the Globe "deeply regretted." But Blair added:

We feel proud [nevertheless] of the noble Democratic support by which it was sustained in the House. Of the whole number of members returned to Congress by Democratic suffrages, only fourteen separated from their friends on this question. Of this number we do not believe more than four or five are thoroughly identified with the opposition, or will unite with them in the policy they propose as the preliminary step to the reestablishment of the national bank.[283]

The Globe had been uncertain about the precise vote because six Democrats, "having declared themselves friendly to the objects of the bill, [it was thought] would support it in some form." The six listed were: Foster, Vanderveer, and Edwards, three of the Democrats from New York who failed to support Van Buren; Mallory and Robertson of Virginia, who were actually elected as Whigs; and Jackson of Georgia, who did not vote—a not very accurate accounting. Furthermore, there were eighteen, not fourteen, renegades, a decrease of only three from the special session of the previous fall. The defection of four erstwhile Democrats from the President's own delegation of New York—four whom the Globe doubtless referred to as being "identified with the opposition"—almost made up for the shift in the votes of six Democrats who had originally opposed the inde-

[276] (February 6, 19, March 26, 1838) Congressional Globe 6: pp. 163, 190, 264.
[277] (March 22, (?), June 21, 1838) ibid. 6: p. 466; 6 (appendix): pp. 203, 232. On February 28, the Globe stressed that the Ohio and New Jersey resolutions did not include instructions.
[278] (March 10, 1838) ibid. 6 (appendix): pp. 180–181.
[279] (March 26, 1838) ibid. 6: p. 264.
[280] (March 17, 1838) ibid. 6: p. 227.

[281] (March 7, 1838) ibid. 6: p. 227.
[282] Ibid. 6: p. 264.
[283] Washington Globe, June 26, 1838.

pendent treasury scheme during the special session. The six were from Maine, New Hampshire, Illinois, Virginia, and South Carolina. The two from South Carolina were state rightists whose spokesmen defended their action as being natural for a group belonging to no party, but whose strict constructionist principles were in perfect harmony with the separation of the government from the banking system.[284] This was an explanation which did not account for the fact that their new position was the opposite of Calhoun's, he being the presumed leader of the state-rightist group. It is quite possible that administration pressure induced a change in the position of the other four. But even if this was the case, the overall 1838 vote differed very little from the 1837 vote.

The impact of party disloyalty on the subsequent careers of the defectors varied. The three New Yorkers the *Globe* listed—Edwards, Foster, and Vanderveer—all resigned, but Clarke was reelected, though as a Whig. In Virginia, all four defectors— Garland, Mason, Hopkins and Wise—continued in Congress, as was the case with Rencher and Shepard of North Carolina and Pope of Kentucky, though not with Legare of South Carolina, who was defeated in the next election. In Ohio, Kilgore resigned and Alexander failed in his effort to retain his seat. And while Casey of Illinois was reelected, his colleague May resigned. Borden of Massachusetts tried running as a Whig for a new term in office, but lost anyway. There is no pattern suggestive of a purge in all this. The situation varied among and within the states.

The *Intelligencer's* reaction to the defeat of the independent treasury bill, while self-righteous, was also somewhat revealing:

We feel an entire conviction that votes were given in favor of that bill, out of mere party fealty by those who in their hearts not only did not approve it, but heartily dislike and despise it. [We rejoice over the bill's rejection as a triumph] of independent spirit over the united forces of party influence and official blandishments and temptations. . . . It is reported, and is believed, that greater efforts were made by direct overtures from men in high places to members of Congress, to induce them to give their support to the sub-treasury bill than have ever been made in favor of any measure pending in Congress.[285]

Since the *Intelligencer* had earlier urged the Whigs to remain united—which they did with one exception (Duncan of Ohio)—the journal can fairly be accused of having the same ambivalence toward party action in Congress as Blair's *Globe* had. Still, the direct reference to Administration pressure is new, and even though doubtless exaggerated, is worthy of noting. We shall never know how many wavering congressmen officials of the Van Buren administration actually contacted. But we do know that the President and

his assistants were not notably successful in wooing back those Democrats who clearly opposed his measure. And it was this last group which defeated it.

1838–1840

Democratic leaders did not reintroduce another independent treasury bill in the third session of a Congress which had already rejected two previous proposals. Van Buren informed Jackson of the delay but also expressed his confidence that there would be favorable future action, presumably after the election of a new Congress, hopefully one which would have a majority in favor of the President's policy.[286] In the meantime, Clay was content not to reintroduce a bill which would create a new national bank, because in his judgment neither popular nor congressional opinion would permit such action.[287] Instead, he concerned himself with the problem of getting a congressional majority. The way to do this, he thought, was to ally openly with the "conservatives," or Democratic rebels:

[Some] are struck by the fact that a cooperation between the Whigs and the Conservatives will secure a majority against the Administration; and that without it the majority may be the other way. . . .

It is manifest that, if we repel the advances of all the former members of the Jackson party to unite with us, under whatever name they may adopt, we must remain in a perpetual and hopeless minority. . . .

It was obvious that their position was temporary, and could not be maintained for any length of time. It was at a half-way house. They must therefore fall back into the ranks of their old associates, or be absorbed by us. And it seems to be a prevailing opinion here to be expedient to avail the country of the services of as many of them as we can get, either as allies or as part of our consolidated force.[288]

Administration supporters in the House and Senate reintroduced the independent treasury bill at the beginning of the 1839–1840 session, with the obvious intent of making it the chief issue of the 1840 presidential election. For the first time since 1832, a President asked for party loyalty on a major issue at the time of the party's campaign for a national election. But Van Buren, unlike Jackson, had six years of experience to build on. Even the state and congressional elections of 1837–1839 often involved campaigning in which positions taken on the bank issues were of importance. Thus the decision of the Van Buren administration to make the independent treasury measure the supreme test of party loyalty in a presidential election was the natural culmination of an evolutionary process. And though the campaign

---

[284] Representative Rhett of South Carolina. (June 25, 1838) *Congressional Globe* 6 (appendix): p. 503.

[285] *National Intelligencer*, June 27, 1838.

[286] February 17, 1839, Van Buren to Jackson, Van Buren Papers, second series, Library of Congress.

[287] (October 9, 1838) Clay to Francis Brooke, *Clay Correspondence*, p. 429.

[288] (December 26, 1838) Clay to Francis Brooke, *ibid.*, pp. 434–435.

of 1840 ultimately focused as much on the candidates' personalities and on the continuation of a rather severe depression as on anything else, it is significant that the period which McCormick calls one of "party formation" closed with the two major parties, now organized and competing everywhere in the nation, willfully entering a presidential campaign deeply divided over an issue of great national significance. For a brief moment the parties' two major functions related clearly to each other: to nominate and elect candidates, but to do so with their prior allegiance on a matter deemed to be of such importance that loyalty was to be of a higher priority than fidelity to the interests of constituents.

Practically everyone agreed that all congressmen were already committed on the subject, even before the discussion began. As Representative Eastman of New Hampshire put it:

Mr. Chairman, there is probably not a member of this committee whose views were not fully known upon the bill now under consideration, previous to his election. In many instances the opinions entertained in regard to the measure were made the touchstone by which the political faith of gentlemen was tested; and upon those opinions depended their election or rejection by the people. For one, I should have been perfectly willing to have given my vote in favor of the bill, without the least discussion from either side of the House; but, in as much as it has been, and . . . is to be, very fully discussed, I desire to state some of the reasons which have operated to form my opinion in regard to it.[289]

A colleague of Eastman, also from New Hampshire, agreed:

The remark of a gentleman of the Opposition made here the other day is correct; that every member was sent here as being either for or against this measure. This measure was before the people in the elections of members of the present Congress.[290]

Then, why did Congress bother to debate at all? Burke, also of New Hampshire, was blunt:

I will say at the outset, that I make my speech to be read by the people—for home consumption—not to be listened to by Gentlemen here; as I make no pretensions to the arts and graces of oratory I shall endeavor to gain the ear of the people, and arrest their attention, by the simple power of argument alone. . . .[291]

Leet of Pennsylvania added:

I desire to state, as briefly as possible, some of the reasons which influence me in the vote I intend to give on this measure; and I desire that, through the committee, these reasons should go to my constituents and the country.[292]

Others spoke of their prior commitment on the bill. Weller of Ohio said: "Holding a seat in this hall under a direct and positive pledge to support this measure, I have deemed it proper to defend it from attacks

which gentlemen have been pleased to make upon it."[293] Strong of New York had to contend with resolutions from the Whig-dominated legislature "that if any Senator or Representative from that state supported the bill, his conduct would meet with the most unqualified disapprobation," but nevertheless said "he had been elected by his constituents with express reference to this bill, and instructed to vote for it, and he should do so in spite of the threats thus thrown out. . . . He was responsible to his constituents and to them alone."[294]

During the long debate on the bill the *Globe's* editorials had a bluntness lacking during the 1838 session, when the outcome was uncertain. Blair wrote with confidence: from the beginning he calculated a Democratic majority. The editorials which followed attacked the Whigs who, Blair insisted, really wanted a new Bank of the United States and whose strategy "is to protract the session of Congress and do nothing. They are laboring to drag the session into summer, upon ordinary bills—to compel the body to adjourn then, without accomplishing the great measure which the majority are pledged to their constituents to pass upon. . . ."[295]

The *Globe* even named certain Whigs—Graves of Kentucky, Garland of Virginia, and Stanly of North Carolina—as the "principal managers of the obstructions and delays of the protracted session."[296] At first, the Whigs mustered the required one-third of the House to oppose any change in the order of business.[297] As late as mid-June the opposition was still successful in delaying House action on the bill, with the objective of keeping it from being defeated by the Committee of the Whole. One hundred twenty-two Democrats were needed at all times to make a quorum, in case the Whigs should walk out and refuse to vote on a motion to commit the bill to that committee. But, "from sickness, and other causes of necessary absence, there has been scarcely any question during the session, on which 122 friends of the Administration voted." This placed passage of the bill in jeopardy. Therefore, ". . . no Democratic member should leave the city until the great measure of the session is disposed of. The country will expect every man to be at his post."[298]

Confident of a majority on the Van Buren administration's most important proposal, the *Globe* was not at all apprehensive about the country's having "before it the broad and distinct platforms upon which the two parties have taken their positions."[299] Blair clearly regarded the Whigs as having been inconsistent

---

[289] (June 2, 1840) *Congressional Globe* 8: p. 435.
[290] (May 27, 1840) *ibid.* 8 (appendix): p. 585.
[291] (June 13, 1840) *ibid.* 8 (appendix): p. 568.
[292] (June 2, 1840) *ibid.* 8 (appendix): p. 515.

[293] (April 17, 1840) *ibid.* 8 (appendix): p. 344.
[294] (June 8, 1840) *ibid.* 8: p. 449.
[295] *Washington Globe*, April 28, 1840.
[296] *Ibid.* Garland was still technically a Democrat, however.
[297] *Ibid.*, May 18, 1840.
[298] *Ibid.*, June 16, 1840.
[299] *Ibid.*, February 19, 1840.

on the banking issue in the sense that many supported the state deposit system they had opposed several years before.[300] Nonetheless, his editorials suggest he eagerly awaited a victory which was to be the result of almost total party unanimity, both Whig and Democratic. The Whigs could be charged with inconsistency, but they were as united as the Democrats were on the issue Blair believed to be the most important of all.

Some Democrats chided the Whigs for not openly proposing what they really wanted: a new Bank of the United States to succeed an interim state deposit bank system.[301] Others stressed the point that the administration had elected a majority in Congress primarily because of the independent treasury question, and that opposition efforts to delay a vote or to blame the hostile majority on "party screws" was false, as most who favored the administration came pledged to support independent treasury legislation anyway.[302]

Still, as opposition tactics delayed consideration of the measure in the House late in the session, the Democracy's first leader became quite apprehensive, and he gave his successor and the party's congressional leadership what amounted to a private lecture on political action:

I sincerely regret to see the course pursued by Congress—It appears that the Republican Party have no combined system of action in the House of Representatives—They have no leader—They ought to act with more union and energy. I regret that the subtreasury act as it is called, has not been acted upon—Now is the time the country will feel all its benefits. . . . Urge my dear sir your friends to a speedy passage of this law.[303]

On June 27, a day after the House finally decided to debate the bill, Jackson, not aware of its action, was exasperated. He suggested specific actions that House Democrats should take in order to force a final vote.[304]

From the beginning of the session the *Intelligencer's* editorials suggested that the Whigs would be defeated. On May 22, it stated unequivocally: "Organized as the House now is, we shall not be surprised if the bill now pass that body, and become a law. . . . We believe . . . that its effect, when passed, will, beyond doubt, be to accelerate the downfall of the Administration, [even though] it has staked everything on that bill." Prophetic words. The leading Whig journal went on to examine the forthcoming election

and stressed what turned out to be the major issue of the campaign:

In the midst of our country's ruin, with cries of distress reaching the executive from every quarter, and ringing in his ears the pleadings of the people to save them from desperation, we see the President stand unmoved upon the eminence of his station, saying in effect to *his party*, "Go on with the accomplishment of *my plans*, cost what they may! Let *my will* be done though millions suffer!" Is it to be believed that, under the rule of a President who thus exercises his official powers much more with a view to the success of a party, than for the good of the whole people, the country can prosper? Give him another term of service to perpetuate the power and policy of his party, and the present generation can never hope to see a return of those glorious times when we were the happiest and most prosperous people that lived.[305]

Or again:

What act for the relief of the commercial, manufacturing, or farming interests has been presented by "the party" in Congress? The only act which the Executive has particularly recommended, and which "the party" in Congress appear to take any sort of interest in, is the subtreasury bill. Is that a bill for the relief of *the people*? Far from it.[306]

As debate on the independent treasury bill continued, first in one House and then in the other, it quickly became apparent that party loyalty was to be almost total. Indeed, exceptions to this were were often made a matter of comment. The *Globe* lauded Calhoun's support of the administration, praising the integrity revealed by his surmounting personal and political antagonisms in existence for many years—involving President Van Buren himself—to support a proposal he believed was right.[307] Representative Griffin of South Carolina, a state rightist, followed Calhoun's lead and supported the measure in the House.

But other state-rights politicians were deeply divided over the proper course of action to take. In the Georgia House delegation, there were nine Whigs, four of whom called themselves "state-rights" Whigs, and three of the four—Black, Colquitt, and Cooper—favored the administration's bill. In a speech which was extraordinary both for its candor and the insight it offers on the interplay between party loyalty and personal or philosophical commitments, Cooper told his colleagues:

When the present delegation from Georgia took their seats in Congress, they were affiliated members of one political family. We then differed, as we still do, on this measure. By consent, our friends at home agreed it should not be the cause of quarrel or mutual recrimination; but that either should carry out his views in the most consistent and conscientious way.
. . . [We] have found it indispensable to differ in the choice of the men who shall be used to carry out our respective views.

[300] *Ibid.*
[301] (Representative Colquitt, State Rights Whig of Georgia: June 20, 1840; Representative Lucas of Virginia: June (?), 1840) *Congressional Globe* 8: p. 475 and 8 (appendix): p. 593.
[302] (Senator Walker of Mississippi: January 21, 1840) *ibid.* 8 (appendix): p. 137.
[303] May 21, 1840, Jackson to Van Buren, Van Buren Papers, second series, Library of Congress.
[304] June 27, 1840, Jackson to Van Buren, *ibid.*
[305] *National Intelligencer*, June 4, 1840.
[306] *Ibid.*, April 21, 1840.
[307] *Washington Globe*, January 4, February 5, 1840.

On us who advocate the sub-treasury, the necessity of choosing a Democrat, became as imperious as that which commanded by colleagues who opposed the measure, to elect a Whig and a bank man. This I foresaw before I came here. It was known that every Whig was opposed to the Independent treasury, and the party as a body were advocates of the bank system. . . .

Sir, so long as my colleagues desire to oppose this measure and take a United States Bank in preference, equally foolish would they act to take a Democrat to do the work.

Foreseeing all this, I told my constituents before they elected me, what rule would govern me; and that this rule would make it my duty and their interest to elect "Van Buren in preference to Clay or Webster; and that as for Harrison he could not be thought of under any circumstances."

. . . Having truly stated, I appeal, sir, to this committee in proof that in what I have done and said here, I have done and said neither more nor less than I proposed to do before my election.

My colleagues and myself, at this very moment, have the same difference in reality which we brought with us here. If there be any difference now, which did not then exist, it is as to men, not as to measures. From this remark, I ought to except two of the six, who are opposed to this measure. Those two have now a difference from me, which did not then appear. But I have not changed.

In regard to our opinions of parties also, the same two agreed with me once in that wherein we now disagree. We then thought it would not do to amalgamate with the Whigs. On this point we now differ. I have not changed. In regard to men, I thought and said it would be better to choose Van Buren rather than Harrison. All my colleagues thought, and so said the party, that they would vote neither for Harrison nor Van Buren. Six of my colleagues now think they will vote for Harrison. They have changed, not I.

So that, whether in reference to measure or to men, I have not changed, whilst six of my colleagues have changed, either as to men or measures.

. . . At a recent convention of those who claimed to represent the party whose nominees we all were, it was thought advisable to prescribe that portion of their delegation who are now advocating this measure. I have searched in vain for the political grounds on which, consistently with their former action, it has been done. I grant their right to make this measure now a test, though not so made heretofore. But in doing it, they cannot escape from the conclusion, that it will be because they oppose it, and desire a bank. I know there are some who did not desire a bank, and prefer even this measure to a bank; and yet, by force of party prejudice, join in the prescription. Against such, and such alone, with justice, I complain. . . .

A difference, then, on this measure and its necessary incidents, has separated the present delegation from Georgia. Feeling it to be a mournful occasion, I have waited to the last hour, in the hopes that those who differ from us would give me the benefit of their views, that I might make available that last hour, as a day of repentance.

But notwithstanding two of us have given them our reasons for supporting this bill, and I have privately requested them to answer our arguments and give us their own, they decline to do so, and seem content to see us go forth in our own way without an effort to convince us. Sir, my own opinions are my guide, but I hold no opinion too sacred to be yielded up to the force of truth and reason.[308]

---

[308] (June (?), 1840) *Congressional Globe* 8 (appendix): p. 609.

In New York, the Whig-controlled legislature passed resolutions which were sufficiently ambiguous to allow Democratic Senator Wright, who introduced the independent treasury bill, and New York Democrats in the House to ignore them. Wright, in fact, began debate even before Tallmadge had been reelected and could appear in Washington armed with the resolutions. His excuse was that Tallmadge was slow in getting to Washington and did not bring "direct" instructions anyway.[309]

In Vermont, though the legislature did instruct its Senators to oppose the administration's bill, the two Democratic members on the seven-man House delegation refused to be bound by the resolutions, as was their right. As one of them put it:

The measure now under consideration, and the one condemned by the legislature of my state, was distinctly brought before my constituents during the canvass of 1838, and the convention of delegates of the Democratic party, who nominated me as their candidate, were the firm and decided friends of an independent treasury, and opposed to a national bank.[310]

Veteran Representative John Pope from Kentucky, defiantly recorded a second vote against the independent treasury bill:

He said he told his constituents that a Bank of the United States alone could regulate the currency and exchanges. When the question was before Congress in 1811, he [examined] the subject, and formed the opinion that they must have a paper currency, either local or national. If the country have a local currency, it must of necessity have a regulator—and that regulator must be a national bank. He voted in 1811 for the Bank of the United States; and he had no reason to repent of his vote on that occasion. He, however, thought, that neither a Bank of the United States nor a sub-treasury should be passed at this session— He thought the people should be left to decide upon it in the present contest—that this contest should be first decided.[311]

On January 23, the Senate passed the bill by a vote of 24–18. Democratic Senators Robinson and Young of Illinois were instructed to vote against it, as was Nicholas, a Democrat from Louisiana.[312] Mouton, the other senator from Louisiana, must have disobeyed his instructions, because he voted affirmatively. He did not give an explanation. The only Democratic renegades were Preston of South Carolina and Ruggles of Maine, both of whom had opposed the measure in 1838. The Whigs were entirely united.

On June 26, the House finally voted to begin debate, the Whigs having decided to end their delaying tactics.[313] On June 30, the bill was passed by a vote

---

[309] (February 25, 1840) *ibid.* 8 (appendix): pp. 228–229. Also, Representative Strong of New York. (June 8, 1840) *ibid.* 8 (appendix): pp. 520–523.

[310] Representative Smith of Vermont. (June 14, 1840) *ibid.* 8 (appendix): p. 549.

[311] (June 15, 1840) *ibid.* 8: p. 467.

[312] *Washington Globe*, January 17, 23, 1840; *Congressional Globe* 8: p. 141.

[313] *Washington Globe*, June 26, 1840.

of 124–107.[314] The only Whig to oppose his party's position, other than the three state rightists of Georgia already discussed, was Alexander Duncan of Ohio, who had done the same thing in the last session, and who would be defeated for reelection before the next session. As for the Democrats, Garland of Virginia and Pope of Kentucky—as already indicated—were unrepentant and again voted against the bill. They were joined by Jared Williams of New Hampshire, William Hastings of Massachusetts, William Wick of Indiana (who was defeated in the next election), and Zadoc Casey of Illinois (who was probably acquiescing in his legislature's resolutions). Four Whigs; six Democrats—party disloyalty had been reduced to handfuls.

The *Globe*, sensing the historic importance of the occasion, called the passage of the independent treasury bill "the second declaration of independence." It added: "This great measure makes a revolution in the government as established by Alexander Hamilton and restores it as established by the Constitution."[315] The *Intelligencer* thought the administration used "odious and detestable" means to secure passage of a bill twice rejected and trusted that the people would defeat such an administration in the elections to be held in the fall.[316] Jackson was greatly pleased. He wrote to Van Buren:

> I have just time by the passing mail to congratulate you and my country on the final passage of the independent treasury bill—This is the final blow to a national bank—It will purify our legislation in Congress and free its members from the continued pressure of the bank lobby members. It is a most beneficial measure in many respects, and our republican members deserve well of their country—This gives light, and strength to our republican cause and a death blow to Wiggery, and Harrisonism.[317]

Jackson was not a good prophet. The passage of the independent treasury bill did not, of course, give the "death blow to Wiggery." Quite the opposite.

In the perspective of time it is clear that the vote taken in the House of June 30, 1840, was the culmination of the banking issue as the chief party issue, something which had been developing ever since 1832. Party loyalty was almost total on the measure Van Buren intended to be the most important of his administration. Ironically, the electorate did not fully respond to such an identification. Harrison was elected president in 1840 because of the depression, because he was a military hero, because he refrained from taking precise positions on issues. Shortly thereafter, when Tyler became president, the Whigs divided even on the banking issue and indicated once again how frail and transitory was party unanimity on any matter of political consequence.

---

[314] *Congressional Globe* 8: p. 495.
[315] *Washington Globe*, June 30, July 1, 1840.
[316] *National Intelligencer*, July 2, 1840.
[317] July 13, 1840, Jackson to Van Buren, Van Buren Papers, second series, Library of Congress.

CONCLUSION

The evidence is unmistakable, then: the major parties in Congress divided, even if unevenly, over major issues—Indian removal, antislavery petitions, the distribution of public-lands revenues, the removal of the government's deposits from the Bank of the United States, and the establishment of an independent treasury system for those revenues. The reasons why these issues, and not others, became in any sense "party" issues are varied, complex, and not fully explained by reference to one or two general factors. But, all shared in common the strong advocacy of either a president or an opposition leader. All also had the characteristic of being national in the sense that politicians *could* allow general and not local considerations to determine their position. Certainly this was true of Indian removal and the right to petition against slavery. Similarly, banking and public-land proposals could be more easily defended or attacked with reference to their impact on the whole nation than, say, internal improvements projects or tariff schedules, whose very nature fixed debate on roads, canals, harbors, and duties on products which were tangibly located in particular places. It is also true, of course, that a banking system of whatever kind—national, state deposit, independent treasury—involved the operation of financial institutions located in certain cities and towns. But the vast majority of congressmen were from areas without such institutions and had to come to a position on banking proposals without the usual guidelines provided by local interests. Not all debate on internal improvements and tariff measures turned on local considerations, nor did all discussion of banking or public-land bills adhere rigidly to a national framework. The point here is that it was considerably easier for Congressmen to respond to pressures other than those from their own electors on some issues than on others. One of those pressures was that exerted by party.

The form which that pressure assumed is largely hidden from view. There is virtually no direct evidence that Jackson, Van Buren, or Clay tried personally—or through selected friends in Congress—to persuade individual congressmen to vote in a certain way. Presidential messages, statements made during congressional debates, and editorials in the *Globe* or *Intelligencer* served as indications that leaders considered certain positions to be of importance to their party's adherents in the House and Senate. Since Jackson, Van Buren, and Clay all had long and extensive political careers, much of which pertained directly to the development of party, it is quite probable they talked to intimate associates, especially those from their own states, about their expectations as to how Congress should deal with various matters. But simply because of the still largely personal nature of political relationships, it is unlikely any systematic or comprehensive attempt was ever made to force loyalty to party on everyone in either of the major parties. Party leaders in the 1830's had a healthy respect for other pressures which operated on individual congressmen, and there is little evidence of either the national or state organizations attempting to "purge" renegade Whigs or Democrats.

It is also clear, as Alexander has shown, that party issues developed even before the major parties were organized on a competitive basis in all parts of the country. Party conflict of the type described by Silbey did not simply follow what McCormick calls the period of "party formation." Such conflict in Congress was concomitant with the development of organizations in the states. Jackson obviously hoped for the loyalty of those who had supported him in 1828 when he proposed his Indian removal policy in 1829–1830, a time when parties were competitively organized only in the Northeast. His policy respecting the Bank of the United States emerged as a party issue fully two years before there was a continuously functioning opposition in the South. That opposition was in fact created in 1834 by the continuing debate over the President's evolving banking policies. McCormick finds evidence that parties in some Western states—particularly Missouri, Illinois, and Indiana—were not fully functioning until nearly 1840, even after the independent treasury scheme was introduced.[318] Indeed, occasional references to the major parties' wooing presumably unorganized and undisciplined Westerners can be found in the congressional debates at least until 1840, most persistently in those over the continuation of the National Road.

The connection between party loyalty and congressional legislation was important. Banking policy was widely regarded as the most basic means of regulating the development of the whole economy which the young federal government in Washington possessed. Currency and credit were fundamental, whether the government exerted a measure of control over them or not. From 1834 to 1840 policy in this area was determined by party allegiance far more than by any other pressures which operated on national politicians. During the controversy over the independent treasury proposal Whigs and Democrats everywhere were nominated, campaigned, and were elected to Congress with their position on the issue known by everyone and with the expectation that they would later act accordingly.

To some, even debate seemed superfluous. As Representative Ely Moore of New York put it:

. . . [Of] late it had become a practice for members to be estimated at home by the length of their speeches; and if a man did not fill so many columns of a newspaper by a lusty language, however destitute of ideas it might be, according to the present fashion, he would lose favor with

his constituents, and on returning, would not be greeted with "well done, good and faithful servant." He deprecated the system as obnoxious; but, at the same time, he regretted that there were but too many who acted upon it, and sacrificed the time and money of the country to their own interest.[319]

On the banking issue, at least, the American political system had attained a clarity, simplicity, and unity it had never displayed before.

But congressional activity, even on this issue, involved something other than party pressure. Renegade Whigs and Democrats were sometimes instructed, if they were senators, to adopt a position the opposite of their party's. At other times, such recalcitrants simply could not accept certain features of the bill in question and voted against their party when certain features of the amendments they favored were not approved. Others were either under pressure from constituents to assume an anti-party posture or had already promised to do so during the campaign.

After 1834, Whigs and Democrats systematically organized for each session of Congress. Party leaders in Congress and editors of party journals in Washington tried to keep accurate accounts of the respective size of the two parties and even on occasion assessed the Whig or Democratic "accomplishments" of particular sessions.[320] But, though continued party activity in Congress was recognized by all, certain issues, by common agreement were not regarded as "party" issues—most notably internal improvements. Everyone accepted this curious situation, to the point that very few ever bothered to explain it. And those who did simply referred to the presumably well-known fact that tariff and internal improvement legislation was not a matter for party politics. This anti-party attitude was even extended to discussions of issues which unquestionably were matters which involved Whig-Democratic divisions. Both the party journals, as well as various congressmen, occasionally expressed their opposition to the introduction of partisan politics into the consideration of banking and public-land proposals, but did so only when such expressions would serve their own partisan ends, i.e., when their party appeared to be united or seemed likely to win or needed defections in the opposition's ranks in order to win.

It is quite clear, then, that party loyalty was only one of a number of influences which determined the collective behavior of the politicians who were in Congress during the 1830's. The debates over issues which did not become a test of one's partisanship— internal improvements was, again, the best example— display these varied influences most noticeably. Presidential advocacy, constituency pressure, instructions, petitions, the persuasiveness of debaters, as well as pressures from party—all have to be examined and

---

[318] McCormick, *The Second American Party System*, p. 322.

[319] (October 13, 1837) *Congressional Globe* 5: p. 138.
[320] For instance, *National Intelligencer*, July 13, 1836.

assessed as factors in the making of each Congressional decision.

Some things in American politics have been cumulative or progressive, that is they have developed over periods of time and have never been reversed or eliminated, though, of course, altered. The acceptance of a legitimate opposition, the development of increasingly homogeneous party organizations and electoral practices, the extension of the franchise— these are examples of political institutions and practices that have evolved and persisted, though not without interruptions and temporary setbacks, to be sure. But other things in American politics have been cyclical or sporadic. They have not "developed" or "persisted" in any acceptable definition of those terms. Such has been the role of party in Congress. Though the general subject has so far received only cursory treatment, it is obvious that the conjunction of party loyalty and congressional action on major issues has occurred rather infrequently in American history and can be explained only if the political context of each instance is carefully studied.[321] Certainly from the outsider's standpoint, one of the most bizarre and distinctive features of American political life is that parties nominate and elect politicians, but then do not regularly tell them what to do once congressional sessions begin. The fact is that partisan congressional politics, once established in the 1790's and again in the 1830's, did not persist as a continuous characteristic of the political system thereafter. And the reasons why remain hidden in the unexamined intricacies of our political life down through the decades.

---

[321] The only general account is *History of the United States House of Representatives*, 89th Congress, 1st session, House Document No. 250 (Washington, 1965). The chapter in it entitled "Party Government in the House," pp. 115–145, provides evidence that the period of optimal party loyalty was from the 1890's to about 1920. David Rothman, *Politics and Power: The United States Senate 1869–1901* (New York, paperback edition, 1969) investigates the subject, at least for the 1890's, in more depth in a chapter entitled "The Legislative Process," pp. 73–108.

INDEX